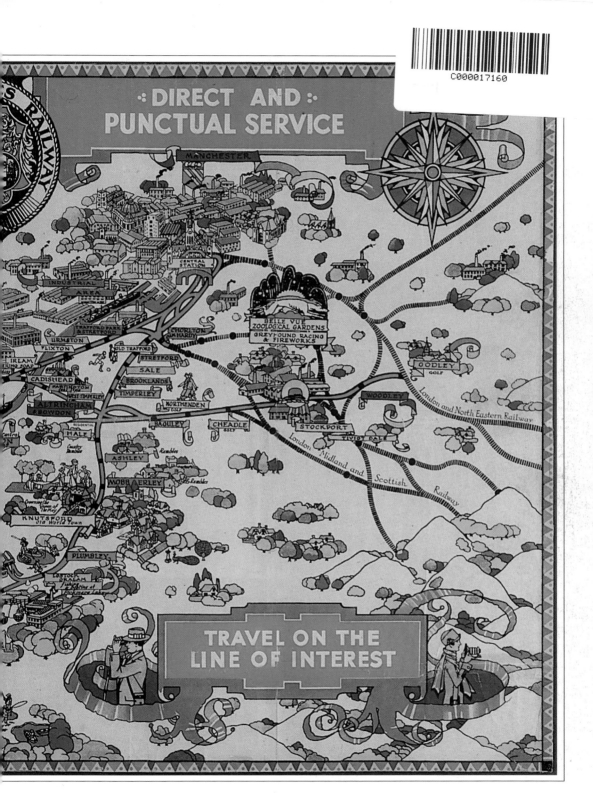

DIRECT AND PUNCTUAL SERVICE

TRAVEL ON THE LINE OF INTEREST

PORTRAIT OF THE
CHESHIRE LINES COMMITTEE

PORTRAIT OF THE
CHESHIRE LINES COMMITTEE

NIGEL DYCKHOFF

Ian Allan
PUBLISHING

Cover: A Liverpool Express leaving Manchester Central hauled by 'D9' No 2303.
Painted by G. Heiron from a photograph by P. Ward

Back cover, top: Manchester United Football Club was a close neighbour to the CLC at Trafford Park. One of the LNER 'B17s' was named after the club. *Dawn Cover Productions*

Back cover, bottom: For a small company the CLC excelled in publicity. This attractive poster was used throughout the system. *David Bownes collection*

Half title: Ex-Midland Railway 4-4-0 No 710 waits in the sidings at Aintree with a special train of MR clerestory stock on Grand National day, 24 March 1923. *E. M. Johnson Collection*

Title: 'D12' 4-4-0 No 431 pulls out of Ainsdale Beach on the Southport line *c*1913.
H. Gordon Tidey/Brian Stephenson Collection

Below: Still in original Robinson GCR form, 'O4/1' No 63722 passes through Delamere on the Chester line with a freight train in 1954. *P. Ward*

Below right: '8F' No 48501 brings a heavy mineral train through Northenden Junction in the mid-1960s. This was a favourite photographic location of the author, who recalls cutting back the bush in the foreground annually, to keep it from spoiling his pictures! *Author*

First published 1999

ISBN 0 7110 2512 5

All rights reserved. No part of this book may be reproduced or transmitted in any form or by any means, electronic or mechanical, including photocopying, recording or by any information storage and retrieval system, without permission from the Publisher in writing.

© Ian Allan Publishing Ltd 1999

Published by Ian Allan Publishing

an imprint of Ian Allan Publishing Ltd, Terminal House, Shepperton, Surrey TW17 8AS.
Printed by Ian Allan Printing Ltd, Riverdene Business Park, Hersham, Surrey KT12 4RG.

Code: 9910/B1

Acknowledgements

Bob Avery, David Beeken, Trevor Booth, Richard Casserley, Ian Clark, Peter Cowan, David Clough, Helen Crowe, Father Chris Dyckhoff, SJ, John Field, Neville Fields, Hilary Gibson, Richard Hooper, Robert Humm, David Jackson, E. M. Johnson, Noel F. Jones, Handel Kardas, Bryan Longbone, Andrew Macfarlane, Glenn T. MacLeod, K.C. Saunders, Mel Thorley, Joyce Vickers, John Ward, David Watson, A. Willis.

Contents

Above: By one of life's strange coincidences, the then youthful author was at Manchester Central on 24 April 1947, casting a critical eye over 'D6' No 2101 at the head of the 12.00 to Chester, when a well-known railway photographer was recording the scene for posterity. *H. C. Casserley*

Left: CLC minutiae; a cast-iron gradient post in front of a signalbox and hut at Risley Moss, all showing signs of age. *Peter Norton*

Below: Examples of the special tickets to Garston for use by members of the CLC Recreation Society; these were occasionally abused by people using them to go shopping, rather than to go and relax, hence the 'Not Available' route note. *Author's Collection*

Foreword

Why someone should have a deep and abiding affection for railways is unexplained. Perhaps the best description of the pleasure given by railways is that of Canon Roger Lloyd, who writes in one of his books: 'The curious but intense pleasure that is given to many people by the watching and study of railway trains, their engines and the detail of their organisation is both an art and a mystery. It is an art because the pleasure to be had is exactly proportionate to the informed enthusiasm one puts into it. It is a mystery because try as one will it is impossible to explain to others of exactly what the pleasure consists... the pleasure of railway watching cannot be explained but it can, perhaps, be communicated and it certainly can be shared.'

I came upon the Cheshire Lines Committee accidentally and unknowingly. As a small boy I used to frequent the lineside at Northenden Junction, once I was able to reach it on my bicycle. When I had a camera, of course I spent even more time there and it must be one of my most favourite locations and photographs taken there will be found in this book. Of course I did not know it then as the Cheshire Lines. That realisation came much later as I began to study railways and to try and find out more about them.

It seems a normal pattern for many people to remember the times of childhood best as the years pass and to me the Cheshire Lines has become more and more important and more and more attractive. That it was a unique railway is without doubt. It developed enormous loyalty amongst its staff and customers, it led the way in many fields and one thinks particularly of its fast service between Manchester and Liverpool and of its publicity. Small though it was, it was an important feature of Northern life and its memory lives on. It is indeed surprising how many people remember the Cheshire Lines with affection and this portrait is an attempt to give an impression of what the Cheshire Lines Committee was really like.

It is a portrait and therefore it is selective and the author's choice. It cannot be comprehensive and a proper history of the Cheshire Lines Committee remains to be written. It is a personal portrait from someone who grew to know and love the railway. Photographs used are not restricted to

those taken before nationalisation, when the CLC finally lost its independent identity, but they must still look like the CLC, which was distinctive and recognisable. The pictures are given space when they justify it, so that they can be enjoyed and appreciated.

The CLC came from the East and headed for Liverpool via Stockport. But when dealing with the major centres Manchester will be taken first, being the city from which in the end the services radiated and the link between the CLC and the rest of the UK's railways, as Manchester Central was where the trains of the three owning companies met. It is also appropriate as it is the home town of Sir Edward Watkin and your author. The CLC had links with many lines, some of which are rarely covered, so we will look round the bend even if under the strictest definition of the CLC the stations or stretch of line should not be covered. The two examples chosen are the Fallowfield line and the line to Wigan Central.

Sir Edward Watkin was clearly the driving force behind the formation of the CLC, which can be seen as a catchment area for his grandiose scheme of a Channel tunnel linking the UK railways with the European railways. He has been called many things and not all of them complimentary, but he was undoubtedly a visionary and he is given a section of the Introduction to himself. So far no book has been published about his life. There is also a bibliography so that readers can explore further for themselves.

A work, even as short as this one, cannot be done without tremendous help from others. Photographers and collectors are credited with the pictures they provided and others are thanked under acknowledgements but three are due very special thanks. Firstly, my fellow worker David Bownes, who has done a great deal of original research. Continuing the analogy of a portrait, he has stretched the canvas, chosen the paints and in some cases done the preliminary sketches. I have chosen the style, selected the colour and completed the portrait. Therefore I take responsibility for what it reveals. Secondly, thanks are due to Bob Miller who is the accepted expert on the CLC and who is the CLC steward of the Historical Model Railway Society. He has checked

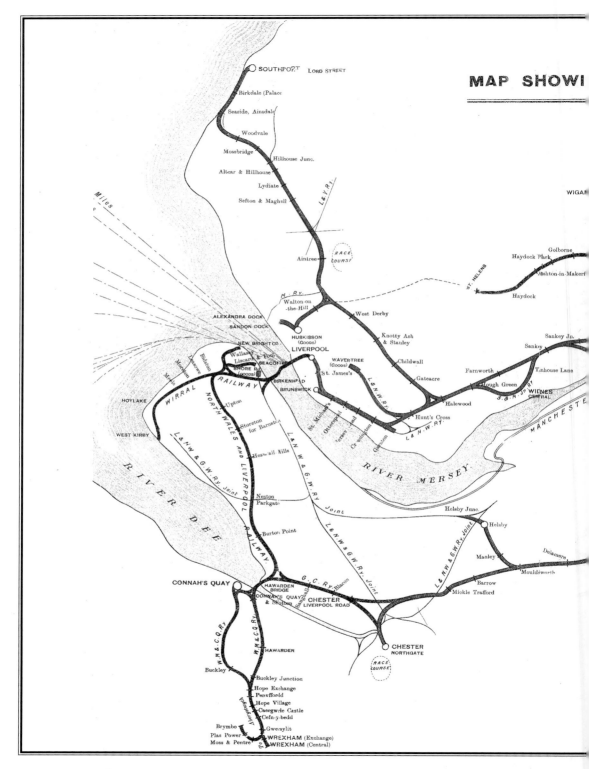

SOUTHPORT LORD STREET

Birkdale (Palace)

Seaside, Ainsdale

Woodvale

Mossbridge

Hillhouse Junc.

Altcar & Hillhouse

Lydiate

Sefton & Maghull

L & Y Ry.

WIGAN

Aintree

RACE COURSE

Golborne

Haydock Park

Ashton-in-Makerf

ST. HELENS

Haydock

M. Ry.

Walton-on-the-Hill

West Derby

ALEXANDRA DOCK

SANDON DOCK

HUSKISSON (Goods)

LIVERPOOL

Knotty Ash & Stanley

Sankey Jn.

Sankey

NEW BRIGHTON

Wallasey

Liscard & Poul

SEACOMBE

SHORE RD. (Goods)

BIRKENHEAD

BRUNSWICK

WAVERTREE (Goods)

St. James's

Childwall

Gateacre

Farnworth

T.house Lane

Hough Green

S. & M. Jn.

WIDNES CENTRAL

L & N W Ry.

Halewood

Hunt's Cross

L & N W Ry.

HOYLAKE

Birkenhead

Mereside

Moreton

WIRRAL

NORTHWALES AND LIVERPOOL

RAILWAY

Upton

Storeton for Barnston

St. Michael's

Otterspool

Cressington

Grassendale

MANCHESTER

RIVER MERSEY

WEST KIRBY

L & N W & G W Ry. Joint

Heswall Hills

L & N W & G W Ry. Joint

Neston

Parkgate

RIVER DEE

Burton Point

Helsby Junc.

Helsby

Manley

Delamere

Mouldsworth

Barrow

Mickle Trafford

L & N W & G W Ry. Joint

CONNAH'S QUAY

HAWARDEN BRIDGE

CONNAH'S QUAY & Shotton

G. C. Ry. Blacon

CHESTER LIVERPOOL ROAD

W M & C Q Ry.

W M & C Q Ry.

Saughall

HAWARDEN

CHESTER NORTHGATE

RACE COURSE

Buckley

Buckley Junction

Hope Exchange

Penyffordd

Hope Village

Caergwrle Castle

Cefn-y-bedd

Brymbo

Plas Power

Moss & Pentre

Wrexhamty

Gwersyllt

WREXHAM (Exchange)

WREXHAM (Central)

CHESHIRE LINES LOCAL SYSTEM.

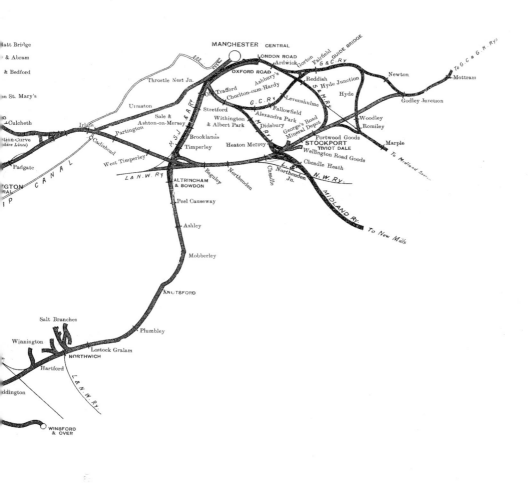

the final text and made many useful corrections and improvements. Finally, my thanks go to my publisher Peter Waller at Ian Allan, who has remained encouraging and patient through the many travails that accompanied the completion of this work.

There are so many others that all I can say is — they know who they are and if I have neglected to mention them by name I apologise. Particularly I thank the photographers and collectors who have allowed their pictures to be used and where known these have been named. One sadness is that many who helped with my last book — *The CLC Then and Now* published by Ian Allan, 1984 — have passed away since then and a double sadness is that so many of their collections have either been lost or have passed into unfriendly hands. It is a puzzle to someone who loves railways so much that some seem to delight in withdrawing material from circulation. They should remember that the taking of a photograph was free and was very often not even done by them. To withhold the image from others is not the act of a true enthusiast.

The last words of this book were written on a Eurostar as it passed through the Channel Tunnel. Sir Edward Watkin might well have felt vindicated in his ambitions.

It has been felt important to refer to monetary value wherever this is known and these references have been given using the conventions of pre-decimal currency where appropriate. Prior to decimalisation in 1971 the Pound Sterling was divided into 20 shillings (s), each of which were subdivided into 12 pence (d); a guinea was one pound and a shilling. The convention for writing sums of money was, for instance, £2 7s 6d, or, say, 5s 0d (sometimes shown as 5/-) for smaller amounts. Obviously inflation has played havoc with the value of money and much thought was given to providing some sort of conversion table. Unfortunately this proved to be too complicated given that salaries were subject to taxation at varying levels, while the price of goods would be subject to inflation, the rate of which could vary between items. By giving the actual amounts paid at the time, readers can make their own judgements. However, it can be said that those individuals who played a part in building up the CLC were well rewarded in today's terms, particularly when one considers their standard of living. Those at the bottom of the pile were clearly less fortunate.

1

Introduction

The Cheshire Lines Committee was undoubtedly the premier joint railway of Britain and the only one to retain its own management down to 1947. By the time it became part of British Railways London Midland Region it had been in existence for over 82 years (80 as a fully independent company), making it Britain's second longest running railway company after the Great Western. The Committee's origins lay in the close working relationship established between the Manchester, Sheffield & Lincolnshire Railway and the Great Northern Railway during the late 1850s, in their common struggle against the London & North Western Railway's near monopoly of traffic to and from south Lancashire and Cheshire. They were later joined by the Midland Railway, leading to a tripartite alliance and the formation of the CLC proper.

In the early years, the driving force behind the expansion of the CLC was the redoubtable Edward William (later Sir Edward) Watkin, Chairman of the MSLR and arguably the railway king of the late 19th century. Under his influence the CLC grew to serve Liverpool, Manchester, Stockport, Warrington, Widnes, Northwich, Winsford, Knutsford, Birkenhead, Chester and Southport. It was, therefore, a railway of both local and national importance, serving as it did some of the more prominent towns of south Lancashire and Cheshire. To give an idea of the scale of the Committee's operations, it is revealing to note that in 1900 the CLC had rail connections with the Great Central, Great Northern, Midland, London & North Western, Lancashire & Yorkshire, Birkenhead Joint, Manchester South Junction & Altrincham, Manchester South

Far left: Sir Edward Watkin was the driving force behind the Cheshire Lines Committee for many years, as he was for a number of other railway enterprises, including the CLC's part-owner, the Manchester, Sheffield & Lincolnshire (which he developed into the Great Central). A cartoon by 'Spy'.

Left: Watkin, the archetypal Victorian Captain of Industry, about the time of the formation of the CLC.
From: The Great Central Railway, G. Dow

District, Manchester Ship Canal and Mersey Docks & Harbour Board railways. In addition, there were regular through trains from the Great Western, Great Eastern, North Eastern, North Staffordshire and Cambrian railways, plus an array of special and excursion trains to CLC destinations from all parts of Britain. On the eve of World War 2, over 11 million passengers and 8.5 million tons of goods were carried by the CLC each year. Indeed, the Committee's commercial significance was much greater than its physical size, which at the time of nationalisation totalled 435 miles of owned single track equivalent and 143¼ route miles, including lines worked by the CLC.

In publicity material, the CLC often styled itself the Cheshire Lines Railway, which despite its tautological nature was preferable to the legalistic and 'unrailway' sounding Cheshire Lines Committee. The formal title was always something of a misnomer, as the majority of the CLC's system, and by far the greatest bulk of its traffic, was in Lancashire. In 1880 Lord Colville, one of the Great Northern's representatives on the Committee, suggested that the name should be changed to reflect this state of affairs. Watkin, grandiose as ever, proposed Great Northern & Western, while another representative offered Cheshire & Lancashire, but as the Midland saw no reason for the name to be changed the matter was dropped. However, the title had been an appropriate description of the parent companies' joint interests at one stage, and to understand these we must return to the 1850s and the circumstances which brought about the formation of the Cheshire Lines Committee.

The railway system of Britain underwent a period of rapid growth during the mid-19th century, characterised by fierce infighting between the incipient railway companies. Parliament was both unwilling and unable to regulate this growth of what we would now call a 'sunrise industry' and allowed larger companies to engage in unscrupulous empire building at the expense of their rivals. Against this background, larger than life entrepreneurs, such as George Hudson of the Midland Railway, came to personify the free market philosophy of the age and wielded enormous financial and political influence. By the

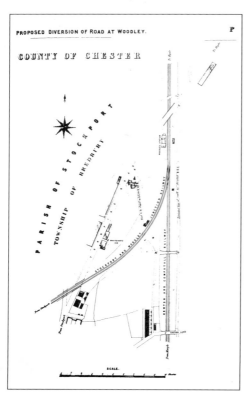

PROPOSED DIVERSION OF ROAD AT WOODLEY.   P

COUNTY OF CHESTER

PARISH OF STOCKPORT

TOWNSHIP OF BREDBURY

SCALE.

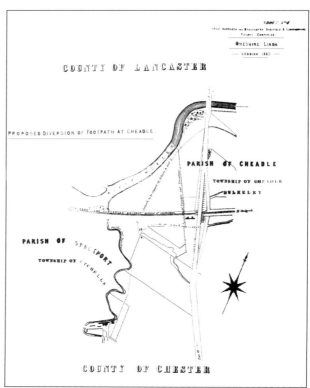

GREAT NORTHERN AND MANCHESTER SHEFFIELD & LINCOLNSHIRE RAILWAY COMPANIES

CHESHIRE LINES

SESSION 1865

COUNTY OF LANCASTER

PROPOSED DIVERSION OF FOOTPATH AT CHEADLE.

PARISH OF CHEADLE

TOWNSHIP OF CHEADLE BULKELEY

PARISH OF STOCKPORT

TOWNSHIP OF ETCHELLS

COUNTY OF CHESTER

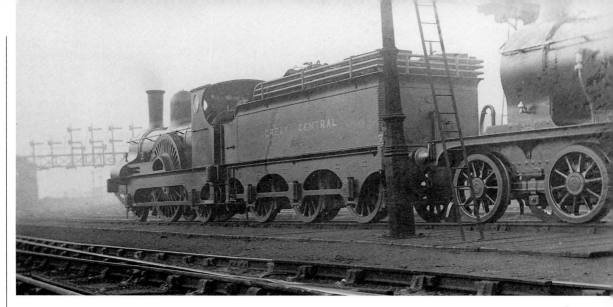

Above left: Plans of a constituent company of the CLC at Woodley and Cheadle. At Northenden the railway went close to Watkin's home; these were the days when industrialists were still proud of the contribution their businesses made to the environment. *Author's Collection*

Below left: Manchester, Sheffield & Lincolnshire Class 14 2-2-2 No 501 stands in Manchester Central station on a Liverpool train in the late 1880s. CLC motive power was the responsibility of the MSLR and its successors until early BR days. *Ian Allan Library*

Above: In the 1900s, with evidence of the owning company's new identity on the tender, another Class 14, this time No 115, stands ready to leave the small locomotive yard that was tucked in beside Manchester Central's platform ends. *E. M. Johnson Collection*

end of the 1840s a number of trunk routes had been established, but with new routes constantly being proposed, the big railway companies were forced into a system of alliances with each other and with smaller concerns which often controlled important sections of connecting railway or offered running rights into the territory of rivals. This system lent itself to intrigue and double dealing, with the more powerful railways able to intimidate weaker neighbours and stifle competition.

The most powerful of all was the London & North Western Railway, which under the leadership of Captain Mark Huish had supplanted the Midland as Britain's biggest railway company and had formed a strong defensive alliance, nicknamed the Euston Square Confederacy. The Confederacy initially comprised the LNWR, MR

and LYR and was intended to protect the interests of its members by dividing goods traffic and hampering the expansionist ambitions of the recently formed GNR, whose main line from London to York had received Parliamentary approval in 1846 (opening 1850/2). The same group of companies had previously entered into a 'pooling' contract designed to disadvantage another rival, the MSLR. Now, in 1849, the MSLR was invited to join the Confederacy, as Huish feared the impact of a possible alliance between the MSLR and Great Northern, the latter of which was known to be seeking a route into Manchester. The MSLR General Manager James Joseph Allport agreed, thus beginning several years of poor relations between his company and the GNR.

However, the MSLR quickly discovered that its interests were subordinate to those of the LNWR. For example, from the mid-1850s the MSLR was concerned at the LNWR's financial support of the Stockport, Disley & Whaley Bridge Railway (authorised 1854) which overlapped with an earlier scheme for a branch to Whaley Bridge from the MSLR's Sheffield main line. Conversely, the MSLR's attempt to gain access to Liverpool via the Stockport & Warrington Railway was blocked by Huish, who made it clear that the North Western would not tolerate any incursions into 'home territory'.

To make matters worse, the Machiavellian Huish was known to have been in negotiation with the Great Northern as early as May 1853, regarding a possible carve-up of territory between the two companies. This would have left the MSLR with no north-south traffic and reduced its role to that of an east-west carrier. All this was

Left: Pollitt Single No 970 heads a Manchester-Liverpool express near Hunt's Cross, c1913. The engine, built at Gorton in 1900, has Robinson alterations such as the chimney; the stock is of early Gresley design. *H. Gordon Tidey/ Brian Stephenson Collection*

made known to the MSLR's new manager, Edward Watkin, who succeeded Allport in January 1854. Watkin, who earlier in his career had served as an assistant to Huish, knew his style well. Consequently, one of his first actions was to implement a policy of rapprochement with the GNR, to guard against the duplicity of Huish.

In Watkin the MSLR acquired a leader equal to the task of dealing with Huish and also of transforming the company into a major railway.

Watkin is the major player in the early history of the CLC and as there is no biography available, this is the suitable place to discuss his life and career. This section of the book draws much of its information from the diaries of Edward's father as edited by a member of the Watson family and from George Dow's three volume magnum opus on the Great Central Railway. The latter book is probably the best yet written on a British railway as a complete business and would be your author's choice on Desert Island Discs. An autocratic character and clearly extremely single minded and difficult to work with, the *Railway Magazine* in its obituary published after his death on 13 April 1901, preferred to call him a railway Tsar rather than the second Railway King. Nevertheless, unlike the first Railway King and despite many failures, the overall judgement of his career is on balance a successful one. The Cheshire Lines Committee weighs heavy in tilting this verdict in his favour.

Born on 26 September 1819, the eldest son of Absalom Watkin, a Londoner who became a Manchester merchant, Watkin's life spanned the same years as Queen Victoria. His ability was noticed early on by his father, who when Edward was aged eight noted in his diary, 'I was particularly pleased with the enthusiastic ardour of my little Edward. If this boy is not spoilt by the folly of those about him he will assuredly prove superior to the herd of mankind.'

Watkin can be said to have started his connection with railways as a child, when the family attended the ceremony on 15 September 1830 to mark the opening of the Liverpool & Manchester Railway. In his early years Edward lived in Manchester itself but contrary to what was written by the *Railway Magazine* in its obituary did not attend Manchester Grammar School, possibly instead going to one of the numerous small private establishments that boys normally attended up to the age of 14 or 15. In 1832 Edward's father paid £1,000 for a house and seven acres in Northenden, which he decided to rename Rose Hill. This house eventually became a grand mansion with pillared porch and large entrance, billiard room, reception rooms, library, servants' hall, kitchens and greenhouses, but this happened much later and when it was originally purchased it was little more than a cottage. However, in 1843 Edward's father described Rose Hill as follows: 'Pleased with the deep quiet of my home at night. We are almost buried in wood. I like the place on account of its apparent loneliness — the depth of the wood in front which shuts out all view of road or dwelling gives our house and garden the appearance of having been formed by clearing a little bit out of the forest.'

Rose Hill later became Edward's own home and the place that he lived in for most of his life. Twenty-two years later one of the constituent railways of the CLC was to pass within half a mile of his house. There was clearly no feeling of 'Not In My Back Yard' in those days; rather pride in the achievements of modern transport.

At the age of 15 Edward was working in his father's warehouse and as he grew up he began to play a full part in the life of Manchester. It was in 1839 that, after a considerable political battle between the Whigs and the Radicals, Manchester received its Royal Charter and became an incorporated borough at the end of November. Involved in the Anti-Corn Law League, Edward organised the operative Anti-Corn Law Association of Manchester to widen its appeal and

Above: Irlam Viaduct was built as part of the new section to lift the CLC route over the Manchester Ship Canal, seen here under construction.
Manchester Ship Canal Co

Right: Unfortunately, filling the canal caused the ground to settle slightly, taking the main piers of the viaduct down with it. This damaged the brick side arches, which had to be replaced with steel girder spans.
County Down Museum Preservation Trust

lessen its middle-class image. He early showed his manipulative gifts by organising a large entertainment for 5,000 operatives in the Free Trade Hall on the day following the original banquet for the people of substance.

These were the 'Hungry '40s' and weather conditions and distress among the poor were extreme. By the winter of 1841 distress in the manufacturing districts increased and, faced by a serious financial crisis, Peel introduced his first budget: to make up the country's deficit he revived Income Tax, which had been abolished immediately after the Napoleonic Wars. While logically it was time to abolish the Corn Laws,

Peel considered this to be a political impossibility and a sliding scale of Corn Duties was introduced instead. This unhappy half measure did not appease the League and from then on it stepped up its campaign. Political troubles developed and in August 1842 rioting began in Manchester. Absalom Watkin had to play a major part in calming down the situation in the absence of the Mayor. Edward continued to have a role as a man of affairs and became a Director of the Athenaeum, mixing with Dickens and Cobden at that time.

However, relations with his father had deteriorated and Edward was going through a

difficult stage. This coincided with his wish to marry his first wife, Mary Mellor, but unfortunately his father's firm, in which he was by now a partner, did not make sufficient money to support both Rose Hill and the kind of establishment the newly married couple would have expected. It was therefore clear that Edward would be unable to marry Mary until he had found another and better paid position and at the end of August 1845 he consulted his father about an offer he had had to become Secretary to the newly formed Trent Valley Railway Company at a salary of £500 a year. He took this job and was just in time to push the wheelbarrow for Sir Robert Peel at the cutting of the first sod in his Tamworth constituency on 13 November 1845.

Edward could now get married and this took place in Oldham on 3 September 1845. A week later Edward started work in the office of the Trent Valley Railway, at a time when the railway boom was at its peak. Speculators were pouring in money and companies were springing up everywhere, with lines constructed so quickly that the map of England was being covered with steel threads. Central planning was as yet an alien concept and government control minimal. What a company needed to do was to attract investors and then submit a claim to the Board of Trade, arguing the case for the construction of the proposed line. Each claim was examined by a Parliamentary Committee to which MPs were appointed. At first there were literally hundreds of such claims and in 1845 there were as many as 20 or 30 separate Commons Railway Committees sitting at the same time in London, causing legal costs to be enormous and competition fierce.

Life was hard for Edward and by 1846 he was paying the price for his unusual energy, drive and determination to succeed. In that spring the Trent Valley Railway was sold for £438,000 to the London & Birmingham and Grand Junction companies, then about to amalgamate under the name London & North Western Railway. As secretary, Edward was entrusted with the winding up of the company and he had to balance the books and pay off shareholders. The task was difficult and demanding and Edward worked for days on end without sufficient sleep or regular meals. Describing the incident later, Edward writes, 'On and after a day in April the shareholders were to call at the office in Manchester for cheques indicating the profit to each on the transaction. Two days before that date my Scotch bookkeeper reported that he was out about 2/- in balancing the books. I replied, 'My friend, the failure to balance even a penny may conceal errors by the hundred. Set all hands to work to carry over every item.' I was so anxious that I sat up the whole of one night and the best part of another. I did not want food and to drink I was unused. A beef steak and a pint of Stout would have saved me from 10 years of suffering and weakness. On the morning of the day when the shareholders were to be paid out, our books balanced. We had discovered errors to the tune of at least one hundred. I went out to get shaved, still without food, and returned to the office. About noon Mr Houldsworth called for his cheque. As I was writing it, I felt as if my whole body was in my head. I tried to write, when with a face as white as paper I fell forward on the desk. I never lost consciousness but thought I was going to die.'

Edward was put in a carriage and taken at once to the consulting rooms of a notable Manchester surgeon, Mr William Smith. In answer to his interrogating look, Edward replied, 'Up all night — over anxious — no food.' In a quarter of

Right: Pollitt '11B' 4-4-0 No 1040 on a Stockport-Liverpool through express in 1903. *Real Photographs/ Great Central Railway Society Collection*

Below right: '11A' 4-4-0 No 875 passes Halewood on a Manchester-Liverpool train. *Real Photographs/ GCRS Collection*

an hour, after giving Edward some brandy and soda water, Mr Smith sent him home and told him to go to bed and not to rise until he saw him again in the morning. Edward slept soundly until 8am, when he sent for his clerks. Soon after Mr Smith came in and whispered to Edward's wife, 'If he does not give in at once he will have brain fever.' Suddenly, Edward relates, 'I felt that I could do no more, my nerve was gone'. Up to this time Edward Watkin had never known what ill health meant. He used to thank God that he was born before nerves came into fashion but effectively this breakdown lasted from 1846 to 1854.

Although rest had been prescribed, rest was completely contrary to Edward's temperament. He could try and cut down on his work but like many

gifted and ambitious people he had made a trap for himself. To succeed in the cut-throat world of the early railway boom he might ruin his health; to ruin his health would shatter his career. The rewards of business promotion were great but the competition was hard and merciless. If he could not work he could not win and this at a time when he had just received a vote of thanks from the directors of the London & North Western Railway Co for his help in the negotiations which had led to the profitable takeover of the Trent Valley Line and its opening on 15 September 1846. Interestingly for our wider story, the necessary timetable changes made it the moment for the LNWR to adopt Greenwich time throughout its system. Edward himself became an assistant to Captain Huish, General Manager of

Left: A fine example of the high standard of CLC civil engineering, this stone bridge crosses the Chester line in Delamere Forest, between Delamere and Mouldsworth stations. *Author*

Right: Study of the old CLC goods station buildings at Warrington, nicely complemented by a more recent fence made of old sleepers. *Author*

the London & North Western Railway and notorious for his unscrupulous business dealings. It may well be that having worked for such a forceful man at this stage of his career, Edward modelled his later behaviour on what had been shown to him. Certainly it could go some way to explaining his later reputation.

Edward continued to be under considerable strain and his constitution could not stand it. He felt himself to be in a vicious circle — rich enough to consult the Queen's physician but it was gaining enough money to pay for the consultation that made him ill in the first place. Edward was able to analyse his state of mind quite objectively and wrote, 'I felt the price I was paying for the privilege of labour and for its remuneration. For I thought of my wife and little babies and the thought roused me to a kind of desperation and made me feel for a time as if I could trample weakness underfoot and tear out and break in pieces and cast away those miserable over-sensitive organs which chained, cramped and hindered me.' But Edward realised that if he fell, others would show him no mercy. It was useless to be prescribed rest, as Huish would have no pity on him. 'By resting I was restless. Unfit to work, I was tormented by an unnatural desire for action. Thus I rushed on with the day's duties as if all the work of the world had to be done in that one day and that day was the last. But an hour or two usually settled the contest. Head swam, heartbeat fluttered. Struggled — knees knocked together — and out moved the cold, clammy sweat which reminds one of weakness and the grave.'

This situation could not continue and Edward became convinced that some functional derangement had turned into an organic disease and that his days were numbered. The Queen's physician, homeopaths, water cure, all had been

tried and none had done him the slightest good, so he decided to have a complete change and to visit the United States and Canada. This was successful and Edward returned in improved health and settled down at once to put together an account of his trip. In both countries he had kept his eyes open and with Edward particularly, no experience was wasted. His visit was but the overture to what he would later look back on as one of his greatest achievements, namely the work he did to unite the provinces of Canada by an arterial railroad. This was in pursuance, in his own words, of 'the great idea to be realised some day, distant though that day might be, of a great British nation planted forever under the Crown and extending from the Atlantic to the Pacific.'

In January 1852 Edward's book about his visit to Canada and the United States was published by W. H. Smith at the cost of half-a-crown (2s 6d). The entire edition sold out. Through 1852 Edward pressed his career forward and he now earned £1,000 a year. Back with Huish and the LNWR, he had been appointed Secretary of the Worcester & Hereford, an LNWR sponsored scheme of invasion into Great Western territory. In 1853 Edward bought a house in London and moved there but he soon determined to leave the LNWR and weighed up the prospects offered by the various companies eager to employ him. He eventually resolved to accept the appointment of General Manager with the Manchester, Sheffield & Lincolnshire Railway with effect from 1 January 1854 or from such earlier date as his commitments allowed. He was engaged for five years and was to be paid £1,200 a year plus 1⅛% upon all increase in net earnings or savings in working expenses, taking the year ending 30 June 1853 as the benchmark. A most interesting example of what we now know as Performance

Related Reward and an incentive ideally suited to a man of Watkin's temperament. Other terms of appointment included a contribution by the MSLR of not more than £100 to cover the expenses of his removal from London to Manchester and an undertaking to pay one year's salary to his family in the event of his death during his engagement.

Watkin actually began to do some work for the MSLR in December 1853, for which he was paid £100, and at a presentation in April 1854 and in gratitude for his past services, Edward was given plate worth £750 paid for by a subscription got up by the LNWR. So with high hopes, aged almost 35 years, Edward moved from London to Timperley, a neighbouring village to Northenden, and began a successful career. In this he succeeded far beyond even his father's expectations and became one of the greatest railway promoters of the age. Elected Liberal MP for Stockport in 1864, he was knighted in 1868 and made a baronet in 1880. He was an officer of the Order of Leopold of Belgium, Officer of the Order of the Redeemer of Greece, President of the Grand Trunk Railway of Canada, Chairman of the Manchester, Sheffield & Lincolnshire, South Eastern and Metropolitan Railways.

For as we have already found, Edward was a man of enormous energy. As well as his work in Canada he helped to build the railway between Athens and Piraeus, advised on the Indian network and organised the rail transport of the Belgian Congo. He proposed a tunnel between Scotland and Ireland and actually began a spectacular pleasure park at Wembley, where the main attraction was to be the Watkin Tower, designed to be 150ft higher than its Paris rival. As Chairman of the Metropolitan Railway he secured 280 acres of land for his plan and the tower reached the height of 155ft before it was blown up in 1907. It stood in what is now the middle of Wembley Stadium.

But his greatest project was the revival of the idea of a Channel tunnel. He was determined that passengers should be able to travel in the same train from Manchester to Paris. It was with the intention of forming a through line from the north of England that he got company after company under his control and inaugurated the Great Central. It is perhaps not too fanciful to say that he saw the Cheshire Lines as a way of extending the catchment area to provide even more traffic for his line to the tunnel. He founded the Channel Tunnel Company, of which he was Chairman, and until stopped by influential pressure groups, supervised the building of a tunnel which still stretches from Shakespeare Cliff for nearly two miles under the sea towards France. Work ceased

in 1882 but the tunnel remains watertight and a monument to an obsession of a most extraordinary man. Yet not an extraordinary obsession as time has shown, with the Channel Tunnel now complete and in operation. How it would have worked in the days of steam is more problematic, particularly considering the experience then gained from the Severn Tunnel. There are engineers who believe that prior to railway electrification a Channel tunnel would have been an impossibility as an effective means of transport.

As well as being a determined and ambitious businessman, Edward shared some of his father's philanthropic interests. While working in the family firm he had pioneered the Saturday half day holiday movement in Manchester and was one of the moving spirits behind the establishment there of public parks. As a railway manager he arranged for each station master along his line was given a turkey for Christmas, he started saving banks and benevolent firms for

Above: LNER 'D6' (GCR '11A') 4-4-0 No 858 near Urmston with a Manchester-bound local in June 1924. The rural environs of 75 years ago would intrigue a modern visitor to the site.
A. R. Prince/Ian Allan Library

the staff and encouraged the setting up of schools for the education of employees. From Absalom, Edward had inherited a strong imaginative streak which in his case was combined with business acumen, courage and relentless ambition. Throughout his life he disliked being referred to as a Railway King, thinking of himself rather as a politician with railway interests.

Once recovered from ill health, he resumed his prodigious work rate. By 1881, which can be described as the heyday of his career, Edward was the director of nine railways and trustee of a tenth. These included the Cheshire Lines, the East London, the Manchester, Sheffield & Lincolnshire, the Manchester South Junction & Altrincham, the Metropolitan, the Oldham, Ashton & Guide Bridge, the Sheffield & Midland Joint, the South Eastern, the Wigan Junction and the New York, Lake Eyrie and Western Railways. His son Alfred, after serving as Locomotive Superintendent of the South Eastern Railway for a short period, represented the Watkin interest in four of the above mentioned lines in addition to the Elham Valley, Greenwich Dock & Railway and the Lydd. As Chairman of the MSLR, Edward never missed a shareholder meeting in almost 30 years. During the period when he combined this

Chairmanship with those of the Metropolitan and South Eastern, he made it his invariable practice to preside at all the half-yearly meetings in one week. Very often Edward would come down to Manchester on the Tuesday by the 2 o'clock train from King's Cross arriving at 6.15pm, go through his half-yearly papers in about an hour, preside at the Sheffield meeting at 12 o'clock on Wednesday, rush off to London at 2pm and then preside at the South Eastern and Metropolitan meetings on the Thursday and Friday, getting back to Manchester at 6.15pm on Friday evening. Clearly as a successful Victorian businessman Edward had completely recovered from his mid-life crisis of health and he then retained his verve and energy for the rest of his working life.

Edward married again soon after his first wife's death in 1888, bought more acres in Northenden and greatly extended and embellished Rose Hill. He followed his father in his love of books and built himself a library that was so extensive that he published privately two volumes: one listed the contents of his library and the other gave instructions on how they were best to be used. He died in 1901 and is buried in the churchyard at Northenden, close to his father, his mother, his sister and his first wife.

Watkin's policy towards the GNR soon began to bear fruit in the form of improved working relations. Even so, the MSLR continued to be associated with Euston, despite opposition from shareholders, many of whom believed that the GNR was the natural ally of the Company. Meanwhile, events were moving against the Confederacy. A court case into the affairs of the so-called 'Little North Western Railway' (as distinct from its much larger namesake) in 1856 revealed the existence of an illegal 'common purse' arrangement between the Midland and the LNWR for pooling and distributing the revenue. This secret agreement had been one of the foundations of the Confederacy and it now had to be abandoned to prevent further action being taken. But there was nothing to stop the LNWR from legitimately working with its old allies towards common objectives. However, with the Confederacy in ruins, Huish saw no reason to honour previous agreements with the MR and in 1857 approached the General Manager of the GNR, Seymour Clarke, with the offer of a straightforward division of territory along the lines first mooted in 1853.

Suspicious of the LNWR's motives and aware of an opportunity to turn the tables on his old rival, Seymour Clarke refused to entertain Huish's proposal. Instead, he informed Watkin of the LNWR's intention and proposed that the GNR and MSLR should enter into an even closer working relationship. In this, the Great Northern was undoubtedly motivated by the prospect of gaining access to Manchester via the MSLR's route from Retford, while, as we have seen, the MSLR had its own reasons for severing ties with the North Western. All earlier agreements between the MSLR and LNWR were declared void, and to mark the new era a joint MSLR/GNR service between Manchester London Road and King's Cross was inaugurated in 1857. The new working arrangements, designed to operate for 50 years, were codified under the Great Northern and Manchester, Sheffield & Lincolnshire Traffic Arrangements Bill (enacted 23 July 1858).

Not surprisingly, the North Western was furious at finding itself outmanoeuvred, and in the months leading to the Bill's enactment declared an all out 'war' on the MSLR, which it accused of betrayal! The war was most bitterly played out at Manchester London Road, where the MSLR shared facilities with the North Western. Under instructions from Euston, MSLR booking offices were nailed up and the company's clerks forcibly ejected for trying to enter their workplace. Similarly, the title of the MSLR was painted out on notice boards and stationary goods trains were positioned in front of MSLR expresses. A price war followed, during which the LNWR attempted to bribe MSLR clerks for information and successfully undercut the MSLR for goods traffic between Lancashire and Leeds, Lincoln and Peterborough. The LYR and MR offered to mediate (no doubt worried by the effect of the price war on themselves) but the LNWR would have none of it.

Hostilities were eventually brought to an end by the resignation of Huish in September 1858, the price war having already been settled due to the inevitability of the GN&MSLR Traffic Act. Huish's protectionist policy had failed to destroy the GNR, and the stage was now set for an alliance between the MSLR and GNR for the promotion of railways in south Lancashire, and in particular a new route to Liverpool.

A peace treaty between the three companies was worked out at Euston towards the end of 1858 and came into effect from 1 January 1859. Essentially, the warring parties agreed to the principle of equal rates and fares, and each company was to make through rates and arrangements for the interchange of all traffic. The agreement should have led to more harmonious working relations but as events were to prove, negotiated settlements could quickly turn into worthless scraps of paper if one of the signatories saw advantage in ignoring its promises. Before the end of the year the MSLR had upset relations with the North Western by supporting several new railways in the Manchester area, two of which — the Cheshire Midland and the Stockport & Woodley Junction — were to form the basis of the future Cheshire Lines Committee. However, in the case of the Cheshire Midland the LNWR had no real cause for complaint as it had originally agreed that this line should be joint LNWR and MSLR and worked as an extension of the MSJAR, before deciding not to be part of this arrangement. By 1860 the MSLR was interested in three additional bills for the extension of its railway in the direction of Liverpool and Chester, namely the Garston & Liverpool, the Stockport, Timperley & Altrincham Junction and the West Cheshire railways, which were also to form part of the CLC and similarly angered the LNWR because of their geographical location. But the MSLR was unable to fund these projects by itself and recurring

Left: A new parcels service van for the CLC, seen near the builder's (Thornycroft) factory in Basingstoke before delivery. The 20mph speed limit sign painted on the chassis is a reminder of the strict controls then applied to commercial road vehicles. *Ian Allan Library*

Right: In well-worn 'NE' wartime livery, 'J10' 0-6-0 No 5143 is seen with a train of empty coal wagons at Bank Hall Lane, Hale, on 3 June 1947. *C. A. Appleton/GCRS Collection*

financial problems earned the company the alternative title of Money Sunk and Lost. Indeed, there was even talk of a possible takeover bid by the LNWR, while negotiations for a merger between the MSLR and GNR were taken seriously at the time.

In the end, the Great Northern, which was just as keen to reach Liverpool as its Sheffield ally, came to an agreement with the MSLR during 1862 over the future of the West Cheshire, Cheshire Midland, Stockport, Timperley & Altrincham Junction and Stockport & Woodley Junction railways. Each was to subscribe equally towards the capital of these lines, which were to be managed by a joint committee of representatives from the MSLR and GNR. The agreement was confirmed by the Great Northern (Cheshire Lines) Act of 13 July 1863, thus marking the first use of the term Cheshire Lines, which was then an accurate description of the joint railways' geographical extent. The agreement was later extended to the Garston & Liverpool Railway.

The Committee's functions were decided when it first met at Manchester London Road on 5 November 1863. William English, Manager of the South Yorkshire Railway, was appointed Manager of the joint lines, then referred to as the Liverpool, Garston & Cheshire Railways, on a salary of £600pa. His career had started with the GWR and English was promoted to Northern Divisional Goods Manager of that railway in September 1857. He resigned to take up the position of Traffic Manager of the South Yorkshire Railway on 31 July 1858 at a salary of £450pa. In 1863 the SYR was in the process of being taken over by the MSLR. Other principal

appointments were Edward Ross (the MSLR Secretary) as Secretary and Mr J. S. Wilkinson (from the Great Northern) as Resident Engineer (soon after replaced by Sacré from the MSLR).

Meanwhile, the LNWR's truce with the GNR and MSLR in 1858/9 had left the Midland at a disadvantage, since it alone had no access to south Lancashire. At the same time, the MR's old 'ally', the North Western, was pursuing an aggressive policy of expansion towards Buxton and the Peak District, which was seen as an invasion of its territory by the Midland. Against this background, the MR entered into negotiations with the MSLR and GNR (with neither of which it had been on good terms previously) regarding better access to Manchester. The result was a connection from New Mills to Manchester London Road (completed in 1867) and eventual entry of the MR to the incipient Cheshire Lines.

As will be discussed later, the Midland's overriding interest in becoming associated with the joint ventures of the MSLR and GNR was the prospect they presented of reaching Liverpool, until then the virtual preserve of the LNWR and its subsidiaries. Powers for the MR to become an equal partner were achieved by the Cheshire Lines Transfer Act of 5 July 1865, which grouped the four jointly administered companies in Cheshire together with the Garston & Liverpool Railway and the recently authorised Liverpool Central Station Railway, and placed them under the direct ownership of the MSLR and GNR. The Midland took up its membership of the Committee in 1866, and under the Cheshire Lines Act of 15 August 1867 the CLC was authorised as a fully independent concern with its own seal and management, although retaining its triple control.

Following the formal entry of the MR, the Committee consisted of nine members, appointed equally by each of the three parent companies. With the triple partnership established, Watkin (who had become Chairman of the MSLR in 1864) could concentrate on his principal objective — the construction of an independent route from Manchester to Liverpool. Indeed, during English's tenure of office as Manager (1863-82), the CLC was used again and again as a vehicle for the expansion of the MSLR. As we will see, the Great Northern and Midland companies were rarely happy with the MSLR's use of the joint railway, and occasionally acted to curtail Watkin's more ambitious schemes. It is also noteworthy that the formation of the joint committee did not prevent disputes arising between the parent companies elsewhere, and it would be mistaken to see the MSLR, GNR and MR acting in unison as a powerful force in 19th century railway affairs.

The principal expansion of the Cheshire Lines took place during the 1870s, with the opening of the extension from Northwich to Helsby and Chester (1870-74), the Liverpool-Manchester main line (1873) and the North Liverpool Lines to Huskisson (1879/80). Other notable building works during this period included the construction

of Birkenhead Shore Road Goods Depot (1871), Liverpool and Manchester Central stations (1874 and 1880) and the CLC connection with the Manchester South District Railway (1880).

William English was succeeded on 1 October 1882 by David Meldrum, who was to become the CLC's longest serving manager. Meldrum's railway career commenced as a junior clerk on the Edinburgh, Perth & Dundee Railway (later absorbed into the North British). Here he gained a general all-round training, moving in succession through the Coaching, Goods, Audit-office, Goods Manager and General Manager's Departments, before leaving Scotland to work on various Indian railways. On his return in 1872, Meldrum was appointed Superintendent of Chester General station (LNWR & GWR Joint), which he held until his recruitment by the CLC in 1882. During his time in office, the position of Engineer-in-Chief was held by W. G. Scott, who had joined the CLC in 1875, having previously worked as District Engineer for the MSLR.

Under Meldrum's leadership, the CLC underwent a period of consolidation, although Watkin's hand was still evident in the overall direction of the Committee. The last of the CLC's major building projects were undertaken during

the 1880s, including the opening of the Warrington avoiding line (1883) and the Southport and Cheshire Lines Extension Railway (1884). The 1880s and 1890s were also a time of economic growth for the Committee, and facilities were enlarged at a number of locations, including Liverpool, Manchester and Birkenhead, the latter being substantially enhanced in 1892 by the opening of a second goods depot at East & West Float in Wallasey.

The range of services offered by the CLC was increased in 1899 following the opening of the MSLR's main line to London (Marylebone). In anticipation of this, the MSLR had changed its name to the Great Central Railway in August 1897, necessitating a number of administrative changes to the CLC's management, including the replacement of the MSLR crest on the CLC coat

Top Left: 'C13' 4-4-2T No 67413 brings the 12.15pm departure from Hale under the distinctive Ashley Road Bridge on 21 May 1948. The 'C13s' were Robinson's first suburban passenger tank design. No 67413 was built at Gorton in 1903, was given its BR identity in March 1948 and was withdrawn in December 1957. *C. A. Appleton*

Above left: A pair of '3F' 0-6-0s, No 43191 in early BR livery leading No 43548, storm through Cheadle with a coal train on a wintry 26 January 1952. Two of the famous BR Cuneo posters, one being 'A Locomotive is Wheeled', are on the noticeboard beside the signalbox. *Author*

Above right: Part of the CLC's success lay in its lively marketing strategy, such as this promotional bookmark produced in 1931. *D. Bownes Collection*

of arms by the new device of the GCR. Cynical investors who had previously given the MSLR its unkind appellation Money Sunk and Lost, now changed it to Gone Completely.

The directors of the Committee responded to Meldrum's sudden death in January 1904 with shock. At a meeting held at King's Cross on 16 February, the Committee recorded, 'the high esteem in which Mr Meldrum was held by all, not only for his business abilities but also for the strict impartiality which he had invariable maintained in their discussions'. In the interim search for a successor, the day-to-day management of the company fell on the Chief Engineer, Harry Blundell (who had taken over from Scott in 1902), and the Outdoor Superintendent, Robert Charlton, who had been with the Committee since 1868 and was described by Meldrum in an 1899 interview with the *Railway Magazine* as being 'my trusted right hand man'.

James Pinion, the former manager of the Belfast & County Down Railway, was appointed as Meldrum's replacement in May 1904, on a salary of £1,000 plus £50 a year for a home. His record in Northern Ireland was exemplary and during his 13 years as manager of the BCDR receipts had increased by nearly 56%. He was also known for his interest in the welfare of staff and brought to the CLC his determination to improve the living and working conditions of all grades of railwaymen.

His period as manager of the CLC was generally judged to have been a success, although from October 1909 to his retirement in July 1910, he played an increasingly remote role in the affairs of the Committee and was never present at the monthly Officers' Meetings. Instead, his functions were performed by Charlton and Blundell, the former of whom became the temporary manager of the CLC from July until his death in December 1910. From then until the appointment of a new manager in August 1911, management duties were shared between Blundell and the Indoor Assistant, William Oates.

The new Manager was John E. Charnley, who came to the CLC from the Lancashire & Yorkshire Railway, where he had served as Passenger Superintendent at Wakefield. In an interview with the *Railway Magazine* (1913) he was described as 'a strict disciplinarian' who, like Pinion, was 'ever mindful of the best interests of the railway workers, and always ready to promote their welfare in every possible way'. Continuity was maintained by the retention of senior CLC officers, including Harry Blundell (Engineer), William Oates (Assistant to Manager), Glegge Thomas (Rating Officer 1878-1922 and in addition Secretary from 1892) and John Young (Accountant since 1896).

Charnley's main achievements were to manage the company through the difficult years of World War 1 and to oversee the transition to new management brought about by the Grouping of 1923. The first of these was by no means easy as, owing to the CLC's strategic importance, freight traffic increased dramatically, necessitating new works and operational improvements to meet the demands placed on the Committee by the War Office. It was during this period that A. P. Ross was appointed Chief Engineer (1917), replacing Blundell who went to the Great Central in the same capacity.

The Grouping was the result of government control of the railways during the war, which had inevitably led to the neglect of the infrastructure in the interests of dealing with the national emergency. Following the declaration of peace in 1918, demands were made for the nationalisation of railways, but the postwar government was opposed to such a scheme and instead favoured the amalgamation of Britain's 123 railway companies into four roughly geographically based groupings. The proposals were embodied in the Railways Act of 1921 and came into effect on 1 January 1923.

During the negotiations leading to the Act, the question of whether the CLC should be absorbed by one of the main railway groups was keenly debated. The most obvious solution would have been to incorporate the CLC into the North Western, Midland and West Scottish Group (which became the LMS), on the basis of its geographical location. However, such a move would have seriously disadvantaged the North Eastern and East Scottish Group (which became the LNER), as it would have severed the new company from the interests and investments of the GNR and GCR in Manchester and Liverpool. Hence, together with the Somerset & Dorset and Midland & Great Northern Joint railways (both of which were to lose their independent status in the 1930s), the CLC was exempted from the Act. The reasons for this were most fully explained by the Minister of Transport, Sir Eric Geddes, in an address to the Standing Committee on 14 June 1921:

'The reason that joint lines, which are owned by the constituent parts of the proposed groups, were left out of the grouping was merely a want of ability to arrive at anything like a reasonable grouping and a reasonable allotment of interest. If you took a joint line like the Cheshire Lines and gave it to one group or another, you would seriously affect

the financial position of the group which is deprived of that joint interest as an access to great centres of traffic. If these matters, as some Hon Members may think should have been done, had been dealt with in the Bill, then the Bill would have been two or three times its present size. It is almost impossible to deal with all these things in the first Bill. That is why the joint lines were left out.'

The management committee of the CLC was henceforth drawn from the LNER and LMS, which provided six and three representatives respectively, to reflect the pre-Grouping division between the GCR, GNR and MR. Otherwise, the CLC retained independent control of its operations.

Following the death of Charnley, the CLC took the unusual step of appointing his Assistant, William Oates, to the position of Manager in February 1925. Oates had entered the service of the Committee in 1881, and spent the first 10½ years of his career in various capacities at Brunswick station, before being moved to the Manager's Office in 1891. He was a man of undoubted skill and utter devotion to the Cheshire Lines, to the extent that he turned down offers of more lucrative employment elsewhere. However, according to one of his subordinates at the time, Oates caused a certain amount of ill feeling by promoting his three sons and a nephew to influential positions at Head Office. One son,

W. E. Oates, eventually became Assistant to the Manager at Liverpool Central while another, W. Hugh Oates, became Station Master at Manchester Central. Even so, he was regarded as one of the CLC's most able managers, and his death in 1926, after only a year in office, was seen as a great loss to the Committee.

Oates was in turn succeeded by A. P. Ross, who combined his role as Engineer with that of Manager. Ross was the eldest son of Alexander Ross, the former Chief Engineer of both the MSLR and GNR, and one-time President of the Institution of Civil Engineers. A. P. Ross began his career with the Engineer's Department of the Great Northern in 1900, subsequently going as assistant to Mr W. Marriott of the M&GN Joint and later becoming involved with the building of the South Yorkshire Joint Railway and the Metropolitan Water Board's reservoir at Chingford. Returning to the GNR, he became Assistant Engineer in 1912 and five years later was appointed Chief Engineer of the CLC.

His appointment as Manager towards the end of 1926 coincided with the collapse of the General

Above: Just east of Northwich, the Chester line crosses the Weaver Canal and the River Dane on one of the biggest civil engineering works on the CLC, a 50-span viaduct. This view, showing the two girder spans, dates from Edwardian times and is taken from the album presented to Manager James Pinion on his retirement in 1910.
County Down Museum Preservation Trust

Strike, which had created severe operational difficulties for the CLC and the worst returns since the 1860s (see below). The fortunes of the Committee recovered slightly over the next three years and Ross made himself popular with all grades of staff, due to improvements in matters of pay and welfare. He has also been credited with resolving personality problems at Head Office created by the ascendancy of the Oates family.

At this time, the CLC's Headquarters at Liverpool Central was regarded as a useful training ground for aspiring railwaymen. The young A. J. Pearson, who later became Assistant General Manager of BR's London Midland Region, recalled that:

'Anyone joining the service there could get some training or experience in most departments. It was in fact a large railway in miniature, ideal for a youngster anxious to learn. The Midland and later the London, Midland & Scottish owned a small railway in

Ulster called the Northern Counties Committee — not unlike the Cheshire Lines — whence it drew a number of its senior officers, partly because of the excellent training they received there.' (A. J. Pearson, *Man of the Rail*)

However, the Cheshire Lines did not offer much in the way of prospects for senior staff and pay was comparatively low, with the result that many of its ablest recruits left after a few years' service. This was certainly the case with A. P. Ross, who left the company in July 1929 to become Chief Stores Superintendent of the LNER. A farewell banquet was held in his honour at the Adelphi Hotel in Liverpool (the scene of many CLC social events), attended by 200 employees from all parts of the system.

He was replaced in November by Sidney Burgoyne, who was given the unenviable task of steering the CLC through the darkest years of the Great Depression. Burgoyne's career began as a junior clerk on the North Eastern Railway. During World War 1 he had served with distinction at the Ministry of Munitions and at the Admiralty, where he was appointed Commander. RNVR, and awarded the MVO and OBE for his services. After a brief spell on the staff at the Ministry of Transport. he took up a position as Industrial Agent and then Goods Manager NE Area LNER, before going to the CLC. In 1932 he returned to the LNER as Passenger Manager and was later to serve as a director on the boards of two omnibus companies it partly owned.

Left: The Cheshire Lines was one of those systems with a history of finding uses for old coach bodies. This one was a well known feature for many years at Delamere, where it served as a bicycle shed. *W. A. Corkill*

His period of office (1929-32) was noteworthy for a number of economies implemented to tackle falling receipts. These included the closure of Padgate, Helsby and Winsford engine sheds (1929) and the withdrawal of passenger facilities from the Winsford Branch (1931), the former of which were authorised prior to his appointment.

Following the departure of Burgoyne, the CLC recruited its next, and final, manager from the LNER, illustrating the extent of that company's dominance of the Committee's affairs. Indeed, of the last four CLC managers, only Oates (who was CLC trained) had not come from an LNER or constituent background. It is also fitting, considering Watkin's influence in establishing the CLC, that its final manager was the Great Central trained Gerald Leedham, who took up his post in January 1933.

Leedham had joined the GCR in 1907 as a probationer clerk. He was subsequently transferred to the General Manager's Office, passing the higher grade examination instituted by Sir Sam Fay in 1909. After four years' experience in various departments, Leedham returned to the General Manager's Office at Marylebone, and in 1914 was appointed Assistant Goods Agent at Hull. On the outbreak of war he joined the Honourable Artillery Company, but afterwards transferred to the Railway Transport Establishment, RE, being gazetted Deputy Director with the rank of major in 1917. On his return to civilian life, Leedham was made Assistant Traffic Manager, Grimsby (GCR), and later became Assistant to the District Goods and Dock Manager, Liverpool, which position he held until his recruitment by the CLC.

In 1933 the company was still reeling from the effects of the Depression, and it was clear that further economies were needed. Together with other railway companies, the CLC became involved in a number of 'Pooling' schemes, designed to save money by sharing resources in areas of joint activity. The main sources of economy centred on the pooling of cartage establishments and in the reduction of freight train mileage. The Liverpool Scheme (LMS, LNER & CLC), was introduced in March 1935 and quickly became one of the most far-reaching and successful in the whole country. Similar schemes were operated at Birkenhead, Chester, Manchester, Northwich, Stockport and Warrington.

Additional economies followed in the mid to late 1930s, when certain key functions, such as Engineering, Estates, Solicitors, Stores and Accountancy, were shorn from the CLC and provided by the parent companies. Nevertheless, the CLC retained its independent status and management structure, albeit somewhat reduced. In 1936 Leedham, who until then had been designated 'Acting Manager', was retitled Secretary and Manager, thereby combining two of the Committee's most senior positions.

On the outbreak of World War 2 the CLC became a controlled undertaking and was immediately subject to the instructions of the Railway Executive Committee (REC). Throughout the war the LNER acted as liaison with the REC on behalf of the CLC, which was regarded as being of vital importance due to its many connections and access to Liverpool and Birkenhead docks. The effect of the war on the Cheshire Lines was devastating, not just in terms of physical damage caused by air raids, but also because of the extraordinary demands placed on the permanent way and goods facilities. Two years after the cessation of hostilities, and with nationalisation only months away, Leedham is reported by the CLC's official historian, R. P. Griffith, to have commented that the CLC was still 'passing through a difficult period' and that its future was correspondingly 'obscure'. It was an unhappy note on which to end the CLC's long and, until then, successful history, although Leedham was at pains to stress the Committee's creditable performance during and after the war and also the continuing tradition of *esprit de corps* which had been such a feature of staff and management alike.

So how profitable an undertaking had the Cheshire Lines Committee been? From the outset it is important to note that as the CLC had no shareholders, all profits were distributed equally between the parent companies. The very first joint lines operated by the GNR and MSLR in the Stockport/north Cheshire area during the early 1860s had failed to show any profit at all. This was to be expected, as these railways were only the first stage of a much larger scheme designed to obtain running powers to Liverpool and elsewhere. As a consequence, they were unlikely to have had much intrinsic value at this early stage.

Following the opening of the Liverpool and Manchester main line, and other building projects during the 1870s and 1880s, the CLC began to show an annual profit, which rose from £21,000 in 1874 to £145,589 in 1886. Gross receipts for the same period climbed from £25,900 to £641,076, while working expenses increased from £238,000 to £495,487 and open mileage from 102 to 136 miles. Hence, during the CLC's expansionist phase, revenue increased in a much greater ratio than the open mileage (150% compared with 33%), signifying the success of the Committee's new services. Even so, the rate of working expenses was very high, absorbing about 80% of gross receipts.

A number of factors can explain the CLC's high working costs. Firstly, as the CLC did not possess any locomotives of its own, the Committee relied on the hire of engines from the MSLR and therefore its train mileage costs were above the normal rates. Secondly, a considerable train mileage, in addition to purely local services, was incurred to make the necessary connections with the express trains of the separate owing companies, which also led to high maintenance costs in relation to the permanent way and other works. Finally, the sheer size of the terminal stations, and the numbers of staff who worked at them, tended to raise working rates above those expected for an otherwise small railway.

However, in discussing the profitability of the Cheshire Lines, a bald statement of net revenue can be misleading, as *The Railway News* pointed out in December 1887:

'The development of traffic [on the CLC] as a local undertaking has been rapid and continuous, but this must be a small matter to the owning companies, as compared with the contributing value the lines possess to the through traffic belonging to the three companies.'

This was undoubtedly the prime benefit of the Committee to the parent companies, completely eclipsing local traffic. Moreover, judged on the local traffic the CLC barely justified its construction costs, which stood at nearly £12 million in 1887, or the equivalent of £88,000 per mile. With the exception of the metropolitan railways, no railway in Britain showed so heavy an outlay of capital expenditure per mile of line constructed.

In assessing the value of through traffic to the parent companies, it soon becomes apparent that not all benefited equally from their investments in the CLC. For the MSLR, the Cheshire Lines was an invaluable route to Liverpool and was used as a means of extending the company's network to North Wales and elsewhere. The Midland also gained considerably from its involvement with the CLC, both at Manchester and Liverpool, and also from mineral traffic to Northwich, although it ran fewer trains over the Cheshire Lines than the MSLR/GCR. In comparison, the GNR gained very little, and it is revealing to note that in 1900 there was a greater number of LNWR trains traversing CLC metals than there were Great Northern. Nevertheless, the GNR had an important freight traffic to and from the CLC (including its own depot at Deansgate from 1898). It worked a number of daily trains with its own engines as well as some specials. But considering the large sums the company had contributed, it was unfortunate that passenger connections were not better. Indeed, the historian of the GNR, John Wrottesley, regretted that the Great Northern had ever got involved with Watkin's ambitions in Cheshire and Lancashire, which, he concluded, resulted in the GNR losing 'millions of money in unremunerative railways'.

Such was the Great Northern's dissatisfaction with the way in which the CLC was run (seemingly for the benefit of the MSLR), that in 1875 Watkin proposed the company should retire from the partnership in return for running rights to Manchester and over the Cheshire Lines, together with 2½% interest on its capital investment. Such an arrangement would have freed Watkin's hand for even greater expansionist use of the CLC, and probably represented a good deal for the GNR, but negotiations stalled and nothing more was heard of the matter.

In addition to through traffic, and as a means of connecting with other parts of its empire, the

Left: Still with LMS livery and number, '8F' No 8745 heads a mineral train near Northenden on 7 August 1948. This area is now unrecognisable, having been carved up for Manchester's motorway network. *J. D. Darby*

MSLR also benefited substantially from the hire of locomotives to the CLC. By the mid-1870s the annual bill for engine hire was approaching £100,000, and even after the 'Ramsbottom Award' reduced the rates payable by the CLC, the MSLR was still able to make a healthy profit from its hire of locomotives to the Committee. When it is remembered that the MSLR also carried out repairs to most CLC rolling stock and with its successor the GCR built far more of it than the GNR and MR, it becomes apparent that its overall share of profits from the joint company were far in excess of the 'equal third' it received as a parent company.

The earlier years of the 20th century witnessed the steady growth in the profitability of the CLC, which reached £218,689 in 1908, although running costs remained high. The massive increase in the amount of freight carried by the Cheshire Lines during World War 1 had a correspondingly positive effect on the Committee's accounts, which recorded an annual average profit of £340,312 for the period 1914-19. However, the postwar recession quickly reduced these figures to their prewar level.

The 1920s as a whole saw a gradual tailing off of receipts as the effects of the Great Depression began to be felt. With the exception of 1926, when the General Strike caused CLC profits to collapse to £1,502, the Committee made an average annual profit of around £200,000, although this figure is skewed by relatively buoyant returns for the period 1920-22. In fact, from 1923 onwards the CLC struggled to make more than £150,000 a year.

Despite economies effected by Burgoyne and Leedham, the early years of the depression-hit 1930s were disastrous for the Committee. In 1930 the overall profit of the CLC was down to £46,397, reduced to a mere £5,736 in 1931. Worse was to come, and in 1932 the Committee reported its first operational loss since the 1860s, when it ended the year £41,034 in debt. The parent companies were obliged to come to the CLC's aid again in 1933 when a shortfall of £15,738 was recorded, although by 1934 a slight profit was payable to the LMS and LNER.

Under Leedham's direction, and as a result of the improving economic climate, the CLC made a remarkable recovery during the late 1930s, so that by 1938 (the last full year before the onset of war), the Committee was able to report an annual profit of £375,350 on gross receipts of £1,719,951 — the highest figures since 1920. As indicated earlier, the immediate postwar period was one of decline for the CLC, which was never able fully to recover from the effects of wartime workings. It is, therefore, inappropriate to concentrate on the latter years when making a judgement on the railway's overall success during its 82-year existence. Taken as a whole the Cheshire Lines Committee was a commercial success, and a benefit to its parent companies, especially following the Grouping of 1923, when earlier anomalies between the GNR and the GCR/MR were erased by the transfer of joint control to the LNER and LMS.

2

Manchester

Manchester was arguably Britain's Second City during the 19th century. Its fame and importance as a commercial centre and showroom of the cotton industry was such that it was known worldwide as 'Cottonopolis'. Even the Cheshire Lines' normally fulsome publicity guides assumed that the city's industrial and manufacturing reputation was so familiar as to make further comment irrelevant. By 1900 Manchester's population had soared to two million, but many of the earlier horrors of industrialisation, identified so memorably by Sir Charles Napier in his description of the city as 'the entrance to hell realised', had been reformed. Previously rural districts of Manchester were transformed into smart residential areas for the city's businessmen, and it was said at the time that Britain's growing rail network was designed to serve the interests of the Manchester business community rather than the people of Birmingham or London. From the outset it was realised that for the Cheshire Lines

to be anything more than a provincial railway, it would have to establish a visible presence in the city centre. Moreover, as with Liverpool, the parent companies quickly grasped the advantage of using the CLC as a vehicle to extend their own activities in the Manchester area without entering into ruinous competition with each other.

The driving force behind the CLC's expansion in Manchester during the 1860s & 1870s was Edward Watkin and the MSLR. At this time, Watkin's overriding concern was to build a new main line from Manchester to Liverpool. In this way, Watkin hoped to escape what he called the 'running powers line', as previously both the MSLR and the incipient CLC had been obliged to use a combination of MSJAR and LNWR metals

Below: Cheshire Lines and associated railways in the Manchester area, early 20th century.
Railway and Travel Monthly

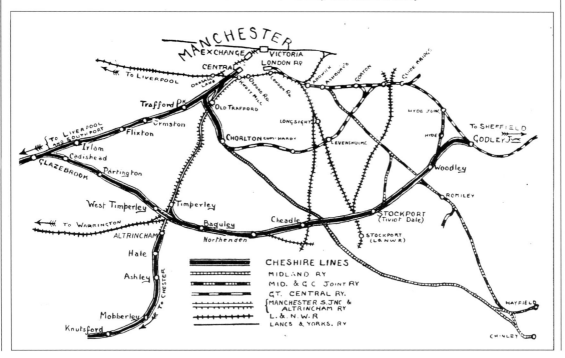

Above: Manchester Central frontage and forecourt in April 1945, with many signs of wartime, such as the blacked-out glass in the train shed, air raid shelters along the left-hand wall and military vehicles (including US forces transport from Burtonwood); but signs too of returning normality, such as the number of cars, none of which have headlamp shields. The size of the forecourt reminds one of the passenger services and administration block and the station hotel, both planned but never built.
Manchester Corporation

to reach Liverpool. This proposal received widespread support in Liverpool and Manchester, where traders were dissatisfied with existing facilities provided by the LNWR and LYR, and from the Midland and Great Northern companies who wished to expand their influence in the Northwest and were thus prepared to enter into an alliance with the MSLR. Not surprisingly, the new railway was fiercely contested by the LNWR and LYR, and also by local landowners and traders on the Sankey Canal. The LNWR was especially obstructive, as the company had enjoyed the greater share of Liverpool-Manchester traffic, and under existing arrangements was able to exert some control over the expansionist MSLR. Nevertheless, the new route received Parliamentary sanction under the MSLR (Extension to Liverpool) and MSLR (New Lines) Acts of 1865 and 1866, and was ultimately vested into the CLC prior to opening (see Chapter 3, Liverpool). This notable victory for Watkin and his protégé, the CLC, was to sour relations with the LNWR for many years to come

and resulted in a wasteful lack of co-operation between the two companies.

As enacted, the railway joined the MSJAR at Cornbrook Junction, and ran via Warrington to a junction with the Garston & Liverpool Railway (MSLR & GNR Joint) near Cressington, the termini being Manchester London Road (MSJAR) and Brunswick. In addition, a deviation was sanctioned from Glazebrook Junction to Skelton West Junction, connecting with the Stockport,

Right: Red liveried 'Jubilee' No 5622 *Nyasaland* waits to leave Central for St Pancras in late LMS days. *J. E. Porter/ Courtesy Railway Magazine*

Bottom: A plan drawn for the 1935 resignalling shows the track layout of Central and its approaches.

Timperley & Altrincham Railway (MSLR & GNR Joint), which was itself vested in the CLC in 1865.

The contract for the Manchester to Garston main line was originally given to Brassey, but relet in April 1869 to Benton & Woodiwiss. As with so much of the CLC's building programmes, once work began costs escalated far beyond original estimates, in this case by £475,000 above the projected figure of £923,000. There were 40 additional bridges and 17, instead of the nine stations originally proposed. Edward Johnson's tender for 16 of these was £59,814 and additional works at them by Benton & Woodiwiss swallowed another £56,032. Permanent way material came to a further £24,000, and work in general was slow due to a shortage of labour and material, civil engineering difficulties and bad weather. Consequently, stations on the new route opened in a piecemeal fashion as they were completed. The

section from Cornbrook Junction to Glazebrook opened on 2 September 1873, with stations at Urmston, Flixton (opened 1 October 1873) and Irlam (renamed Irlam & Cadishead, August 1879). Glazebrook itself opened on 1 September 1873, together with stations on the Stockport deviation at Cadishead (closed 1879), Partington (opened May 1874) and West Timperley.

From the opening of the railway, it was apparent to all three partners in the CLC that better station accommodation was required than that available at London Road. Yet the alternative of building a new terminus in the city centre was bound to be expensive, both in land costs and construction, as it would have to be served by an extension carried almost entirely on bridges and arches. A far cheaper solution would have been to improve existing facilities at London Road, but the LNWR (as joint owners of the MSJAR) would have none of this, thus forcing the CLC to look

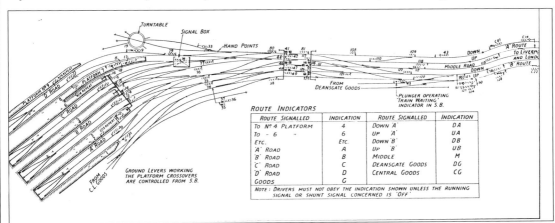

elsewhere and inadvertently opening the way for the Joint Company to run a more competitive service to Liverpool.

An appropriate site was found near to the Free Trade Hall, and Parliamentary approval for an extension, totalling 1 mile 19 chains of double track, from Cornbrook West Junction to Manchester Central station was granted on 22 July 1872. As construction was expected to take four years, it was agreed to build a temporary station in Windmill Street (adjacent to Central) at a cost of £14,000, on the understanding that it would later be converted to a goods station. Manchester 'temporary Central' opened on 9 July 1877 and consisted of two platforms of 600ft and 500ft, with two intermediate tracks for standage. An immediate result of the new extension was the introduction of an improved hourly express between Manchester and Liverpool Central, calling at Warrington only. The service was an instant success, with earnings for the first week recorded at £1,912, against running costs of only £243. Local services were also enhanced by the construction of a double line between Old Trafford Junction on the MSJAR and Cornbrook West Junction, which enabled Chester trains to be diverted from Oxford Road (their original starting point) to Central. The new route was opened in July 1878, although trains to Northwich and Chester continued to use MSJAR metals from Old Trafford to Altrincham.

Manchester Central proper was designed and constructed by the Cheshire Lines' resident engineer, Mr H. L. Moorson. The station had two storeys, the lower being a goods station, built on brick arches with ribs terminating just below platform level on large anchor plates bolted to masonry footings. This was served by rail via a wagon hoist. Externally, Central closely resembled St Pancras, being constructed of a single glazed span of 210ft rising to a height of 90ft above rail level. When the station opened on 1 July 1880, it had eight platforms (increased to nine on 1 April 1906), and was universally regarded as the finest station in Manchester.

However, the station forecourt and passenger facilities were less impressive. The temporary wooden booking offices, waiting rooms and staff rooms were, in fact, never replaced, and apart from detracting from the overall appearance of the station, severely restricted the circulating area within the building. Similarly, the large forecourt, originally earmarked for either the new headquarters of the CLC or for a hotel, remained empty and was later used as an unnecessarily spacious car park. A suitably impressive and luxurious hotel was eventually opened by the Midland Railway at a cost of £1 million in 1903, but sited opposite Central across a busy road.

The station's Refreshment Rooms, like those at Liverpool Central, Warrington, Stockport and later Southport, were leased to Spiers & Pond. This arrangement continued until 1906 when the franchise was taken over by the Great Northern Railway and thereafter rotated between the parent

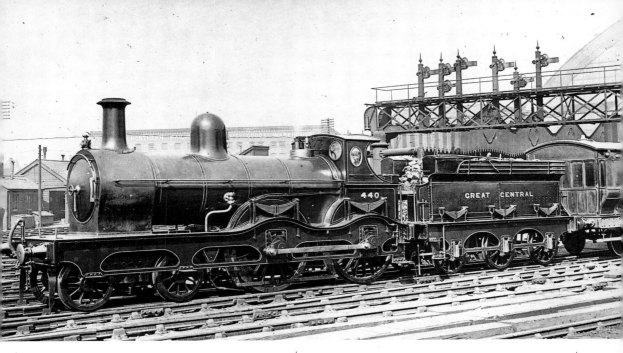

Above left: GCR '12A' 2-4-0 No 169B stands near the original Central 'B' signalbox, the biggest mechanical box on the CLC, c1914. The 'B' in the locomotive number indicates that it has been relegated to the Duplicate List, usually a sign of approaching withdrawal. *Real Photographs/GCRS Collection*

Above: Sacré '6B' 4-4-0 No 440 at Central in the 1900s. The big GNR Deansgate goods warehouse is in the background. On the platform canopy valances can be seen the typical CLC two-colour paint scheme. The signal gantry, which lasted for many years, was an unusual feature on the CLC.
Ian Allan Library/Bucknall Collection

companies. By 1905, the passenger station employed over 300 men under the direction of the then Station Master, Mr W. Kirk. A further 300 were employed in the goods station, which received merchandise from the station by means of nine hydraulic cranes, one of which was capable of lifting 20 tons while the others had a capacity of 1½ tons each. Further goods facilities were provided at the old temporary station, which was converted from passenger use in 1880 by R. Neil & Sons, and at Cornbrook, where extensive sidings and a handling station were opened in 1881. Both of these were served by engines stabled at Cornbrook shed, which came into operation during January 1880. An additional goods warehouse was added at Central in December 1882.

With the opening of Central, it was imperative for the credibility of the Cheshire Lines to maintain a passenger service which justified so impressive a station. As we have already seen, the extension to Central enabled the Company to offer an improved service between Liverpool and Manchester (via Warrington), and it was this express service which became the focus of the CLC's efforts to establish itself as a major railway company in the Northwest. It was clear that the trains had to be punctual, speedy and frequent if it was to compete with those of the LYR and LNWR, the latter of which boasted a fastest time of 50min, although few existing services completed the journey in under an hour. In this the CLC was fortunate to possess a new route which was relatively level, straight and free from too many places where an adverse signal might be expected. Moreover, the Cheshire Lines had the supreme advantage of running trains between two terminal stations, whereas rival expresses to Liverpool had to come into Manchester from points of origin such as London, Leeds, York and Hull, and so were exposed to the potential of many more delays. Train loadings on the Manchester-Liverpool express were also closely regulated by the CLC to prevent slow running, and local and goods services timetabled to avoid interference.

The resulting running times were spectacular by contemporary standards. The 34-mile journey took only 45min, with Manchester to Warrington achieved in 18min. These figures were all the

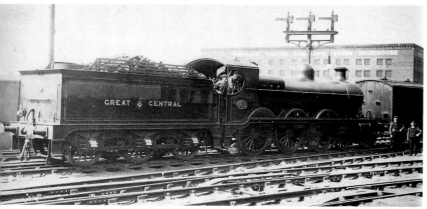

Left: A rarity at Central; in fact GNR locomotives were the least seen of the owning partners' stock on the CLC, although at times regular services were operated into Central. Ivatt 4-4-0 No 1306 is in Central's basic loco yard for servicing. The standard of locomotive cleaning that was then normal shows in the polish patterns on the paintwork. Sadly the duty that brought No 1306 to Central is not recorded.
E. M. Johnson Collection

Centre left: GCR No 184, one of Robinson's '8' class 4-6-0 'Fish engines', in Central's goods yard with a Midland Railway van, with the GNR warehouse behind it. The class was designed for fast working of perishable goods, hence the nickname.
E. M. Johnson Collection

Below: In early LNER condition, Class C13 4-4-2T No 18 stands on shed at Trafford Park, *c*1924. The 'CLC Special Train' headboard is of interest.
Real Photographs/ GCRS Collection

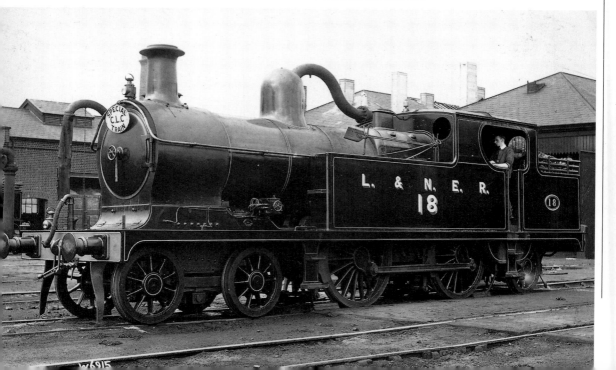

more remarkable as they relied on an average speed of 52½ mph being reached over a relatively short distance. With the opening of the Warrington 'straight line' in 1883, a nonstop service was introduced which took a further 5min off travelling time. Frequency was also ensured, as a daily service of 26 expresses left either terminus at half past every hour from 8.30am to 9.30pm. Consequently, the CLC's Liverpool-Manchester Express became a byword for speed and reliability, and was rightly known as 'the punctual route'. Indeed it was then and for some time the fastest all-year regular express service in the world.

The CLC was also the first company to introduce cheap fares between Liverpool and Manchester, and in 1877 standard return fares were cut to 8s for first class, 6s for second, and 4s 6d for third. These prices, already low enough to give the LNWR and LYR cause for concern, were further reduced before the end of the century to 5s 6d first class and 2s 9d for third. The scheme proved so popular that Watkin tried, unsuccessfully, to persuade his partners in the CLC to inaugurate a half-hourly service. Even so, by 1900 passenger traffic between the two cities

on the CLC was equal to the combined totals of the LYR and LNWR. In 1904 the LYR struck back with a 40min express from Manchester Victoria to Liverpool Exchange. Similarly, the LNWR ran some trains between Manchester Exchange and Lime Street in 40min, but the Cheshire Lines service remained the most popular due to its unfaltering reputation for punctuality.

The predominance of the CLC's Liverpool-Manchester express was, however briefly, threatened by a scheme for a monorail link between the two cities devised by Mr Behr, the engineer of the Listowel & Ballybunion monorail in Ireland. Despite opposition from an unlikely alliance of the CLC, MR, GNR, GCR, LYR, and LNWR, the monorail was authorised on 17 August 1901 to run from a point near Deansgate, Manchester, to School Lane in Liverpool, with most of its route running parallel with the Cheshire Lines. Thankfully for the future prosperity of the CLC, interest in the potential of monorail systems was short lived, and plans to begin construction were eventually dropped.

A more successful scheme, initially involving all three of the CLC partners, was the Manchester & South District Railway (MSDR), which was to provide a rail link from Manchester Central to the southern approaches to the city. The MSDR was originally promoted by a group of local landowners supported by the Midland Railway, itself motivated to gain its own route into Manchester and so escape the cramped conditions it shared with the MSLR and LNWR at London Road. In 1873 the MSDR was authorised to build a line from Throstle Nest Junction (CLC) to

Below: One of the classic pictures of the CLC, this view of Trafford Park Shed features a fine line-up of GCR motive power. The sheer size of the shed is evident from the frontage and the number of smoke jacks on the roofs.
Ian Allan Library/Bucknall Collection

Left: Trafford Park in the early 1930s, with the CLC building plaque proudly displayed above the doors. 'B8' 4-6-0 No 5445 waits for its next duty. The 'Glenalmonds' (named after the first of the class) were Robinson's goods version of his 'Sir Sams'. Generally used by the LNER on the GE Division, they were regularly appearing on King's Cross-Manchester freights at this time.
G. M. Shultz/
E. M. Johnson Collection

Alderley (LNWR). Under pressure from the MSLR to quit London Road, and conscious of the CLC's developments in central Manchester, the Midland pushed for joint ownership of the MSDR and under the MR (Further Powers) Act of 1876 the Manchester South District line was vested into the Sheffield and Midland Joint Committee (MSLR & MR). However, the MSLR soon lost interest in the scheme and in the following year these powers were vested into the MR solely, with provision for the admission of the GNR at a later date, in which case the MSDR would be transferred to the CLC. In the event, these powers were never exercised and the new company became part of the Midland Railway.

The section from Throstle Nest Junction (later Throstle Nest East Junction) to Heaton Mersey opened on 1 January 1880 and connected with the CLC line to Stockport, with stations at Chorlton-cum-Hardy, Withington, Didsbury and Heaton Mersey. A local service of 14 passenger trains was inaugurated between Manchester 'temporary Central' and Stockport Tiviot Dale, with one goods train run in each direction from Stockport Wellington Road Goods Station (CLC). By August 1880, the Midland had 26 departures using Central via this route, including 14 South District locals and 12 trains for Derby, Nottingham, Leicester and London — services to the latter having been permanently transferred from London Road. An odd side-effect of the MSDR's early links with the MSLR was that stations on the eight-mile stretch from Central to Stockport were outwardly of MSLR/CLC design rather than MR descent, even down to the pattern of gas lamp posts. Working of the South District was made considerably easier in January 1889 by

the opening of the new CLC engine shed at Heaton Mersey, which was occupied jointly by the MSLR and MR. MR engines were later allocated at Trafford Park from 1895.

An important junction with the MSLR's Fairfield Branch to Sheffield was made with the MSDR at Chorlton in May 1892. As a consequence of the work involved, the northern portion of the South District line from Chorlton Junction to Throstle Nest Junction (including Chorlton-cum-Hardy station) was transferred to CLC ownership in 1891, authority having been obtained under the MSLR (Additional Powers) Act 1887. From henceforth the 2 miles 3 chains from Throstle Nest to Chorlton Junction was known by the CLC as the Chorlton Branch. The final element in the Midland's approach to Manchester was the construction of its direct line to bypass Marple and Stockport Tiviot Dale. The first section opened in 1901 from Heaton Mersey to Cheadle Heath, and the remainder in 1902. In retrospect it would seem that Watkin seriously underestimated the role the MSDR would play in the development of suburbs such as Didsbury, which grew by 60% following the opening of the railway in 1891. Many of the areas served by the South District became the favoured residential areas of cotton merchants and businessmen and it was unfortunate that this railway was not incorporated into the CLC from the outset.

With the completion of the Midland's approach to Manchester and the diversion of MSLR trains to Central from London Road, the CLC terminus became one of the busiest stations in the north of England. By 1905 the number of passenger trains using Central was more than double that of Euston and St Pancras combined, with 229 departures and 215 arrivals dealt with each day. In addition to the services outlined above, the Midland ran trains to Sheffield, Birmingham and Bristol, while the Great Central offered expresses to London (Marylebone), Sheffield (Victoria) and local services to Wigan and St Helens via Glazebrook West Junction (which opened for passengers in 1884). In contrast the Great Northern's solitary gain from the new station was a through service to London (King's Cross), which combined passengers from called at Cambridge, Hitchin, Spalding, Peterborough, Stamford, Skegness, Boston, Grantham, Newark and Retford, before joining the GCR main line to Central via Sheffield and Godley. However, it continued to benefit from through trains to Aberystwyth (Cambrian), Harwich (GC) and Hull (GC).

In terms of purely CLC traffic, regular expresses and stopping services were provided to Southport following the opening of its extension to Lord Street in 1884. A frequent service was also put on to Irlam and Warrington, from where local trains could be picked up to Liverpool. A consequence of this service was the growth of Urmston and Flixton, which rapidly developed into high class residential areas for Manchester commuters. In January 1904 a new station was added at Trafford Park (& Stretford) to serve the recently opened trading estate. A very large number of local services was also available from Central to Stockport Tiviot Dale, Northwich and Chester, which enabled the CLC to run through trains to the eastern counties, the Midlands and part of North and Central Wales.

Meanwhile the volume of goods dealt with at Manchester had risen considerably because of the increased use made of the CLC's facilities by the parent companies. The CLC had also developed in order to serve local industries, such as the steel works at Partington and Irlam, more effectively. However, the most significant development for goods traffic was the authorisation of the Manchester Ship Canal (MSC) in 1885 which, for the first time, gave the city its own docks and direct access to the port of Liverpool. The scheme had met with vigorous opposition from all three CLC partners, the LNWR, LYR and the City of Liverpool, who viewed the canal as a serious threat to their prosperity. Perhaps surprisingly, opposition from the CLC itself was never as pronounced as that of other companies, despite the fact that the proposed course of the MSC involved the Cheshire Lines in difficult diversion works. Indeed, it is noticeable that the CLC was the first railway to provide a direct link with the Ship Canal and it may be presumed that the company which lacked significant dock facilities in Liverpool was also the first to recognise its potential for increasing goods traffic, rather than regarding it simply as a negative threat.

During the construction of the canal, the CLC main line between Irlam and Flixton and the Glazebrook-Stockport line between Cadishead and Partington had to be raised and diverted to cross it. To avoid interruption, deviation lines were built, while at Irlam a new station was erected on a level much higher than the previous one, positioned on the opposite side of the old line, which remained to pass the rear of the building. Two new viaducts were also constructed to cross the canal at Irlam and Partington, each having a central span of 120ft. Those portions of the CLC which were abandoned in the process became the property of the MSC, which incorporated them into its own railway system serving the docks. The new lines were opened respectively for goods on 9 January and 27 February and for passengers on 26 March and 29 May 1893.

As already indicated, the Cheshire Lines was the first to give a rail connection with the Ship Canal docks. A single line from Cornbrook Goods was authorised in April 1890 and opened in 1893 to assist the contractor with the supply of construction materials for the docks. Although of 'temporary' construction (the line was carried on wooden trestles) it remained in use following the opening of the MSC in 1894. It was finally replaced in 1904 by a new link serving both the docks and Trafford Park industrial estate, which joined the main line at Trafford Park Junction. Here extensive sidings were put in for the purpose of exchanging traffic with the Ship Canal, and by means of Bridgewater Junction the CLC succeeded in serving the whole of Salford and Pomona Docks. The old line from Cornbrook was dismantled the following year to make way for the Throstle Nest South Junction to Trafford Park Junction curve, which thus connected the docks and Trafford Park estate with the GCR and MR main lines via the Chorlton-cum-Hardy branch. The opening of the curve on 1 October 1906 also gave South District trains a more direct route to Liverpool and the westerly section of the CLC. Additional junctions with the MSC Railway were at Glazebrook East and Partington, where the MSC had taken over the original CLC route following the completion of the deviation lines mentioned above.

The importance of Manchester as an industrial centre, coupled with the opening of the Ship Canal and the increasing role of the CLC as a carrier, led the Great Northern Railway to construct its own goods warehouse at Deansgate, which became the company's only direct connection with the Cheshire Lines. The

warehouse, more properly called the GNR Goods Station, was reached by a short branch carried on bridges and arches to a junction with the Liverpool-Manchester main line outside Central station. It cost in the region of £1 million to construct and when completed in July 1898 was regarded as the most advanced railway goods exchange in Britain. The upper storey consisted of 10 roads served by the branch, with a further two roads (one on either side) dropping steeply to the lower deck. The station also had the ability to take goods directly from the MSC, via an underground waterway, to railway wagons using hydraulic machines. A large volume of traffic was quickly established, and the GNR ran a number of goods trains between Deansgate and King's Cross using the Great Central route via Penistone and also over the MR line via Cheadle Heath to Codnor Park.

The post-Grouping era witnessed the continued growth of Central as a passenger station, while Manchester, with its theatres, shops and amusements, remained a popular destination for excursion traffic. In common with other companies, the Cheshire Lines sought to encourage such traffic with the use of reduced fares for off-peak journeys and public holidays. For example, during the August Bank Holiday of 1926, standard return fares to Manchester were

Above: 'Sir Sam' No 5425 *City of Manchester* leaves Wilbraham Road station on the Fallowfield Loop with a train of six-wheel stock on a Manchester-Guide Bridge stopping service. Local services on 'the branch' were a favoured turn for running in locomotives just released by Gorton Works.
William Lees

Below: Manchester United was provided with its own station and special services at match times.
David Bownes Collection

reduced to 2s 5d from Northwich and 4s 3d from Chester. The Liverpool-Manchester express also continued to flourish, and in 1930 an additional stop was added at Farnworth to those trains calling at Warrington. New coaching stock designed by Sir Nigel Gresley was introduced to the service in 1937, with a trial run organised between Manchester Central and Liverpool on Friday

CHESHIRE LINES RAILWAY

FOOTBALL
(ASSOCIATION & RUGBY)
Season—August, 1937, to May, 1938, inclusive

Cheap Return Tickets

Third Class—Single Fare

First Class—Approximately 50% above Third Class Fare

(plus fractions of a penny)

are issued at any CHESHIRE LINES Station to Stations shewn on the back hereof on SATURDAYS and other special dates.

AVAILABILITY

OUTWARD.	RETURN.
By Any Train at or after 9 0 a.m. up to 3 0 p.m. inclusive. In connection with Evening Matches, available between the hours of 9 0 a.m. and 6 0 p.m.	By Any Train at or after 3 0 p.m. on day of issue only.

EXCEPTIONS.

2 0 p.m., Manchester (C.) to Warrington and Liverpool.	2 20 p.m., Liverpool to Warrington and Manchester.
2 18 p.m., Warrington to Liverpool.	2 44 p.m., Warrington to Manchester.

In the event of fixtures being re-arranged or Matches having to be replayed on a date not shewn on this Bill, the cheap facilities will apply to the point and on the date at which the re-arranged or re-played match takes place.

Conditions of issue of Excursion Tickets and other Reduced Fare Tickets:—Excursion and Tickets at Fares less than the ordinary fares are issued subject to the notices and conditions in the Committee's current Time Tables.

CENTRAL STATION, LIVERPOOL.   G. LEEDAM,
August, 1937.   Secretary & Manager.

Above: Manchester United football club was a close neighbour of the CLC at Trafford Park. One of the LNER 'B17' 4-6-0s, No 2862, was named after the club and this commercial postcard of a painting shows it passing the stadium.
Dawn Cover Productions

Left: The CLC made the most of its proximity to sports grounds, as this 1937 poster shows.
David Bownes Collection

Below: 0-6-2T No 69304 passes Trafford Park in more mundane style in June 1949. *H. C. Casserley*

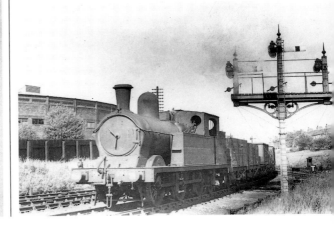

9 April 1937 and in the same year, cheap excursions between the two cities were offered for evening travel from both Farnworth and Warrington to Manchester, the cost of a third class return being 2s 1d and 1s 7d respectively.

Two new CLC stations were opened in the Manchester area during the 1930s. The first was at Chassen Road, situated midway between Flixton and Urmston, which came into operation on 10 September 1934. The second was at Old Trafford, which opened on 21 August 1935, at the instigation of Manchester United FC, to serve the football ground. It consisted of a single platform and wooden halt, situated on the up side of the main line at Warwick Road. At the time, it was one of the few railway stations in Britain serving a football stadium directly, and on match days a shuttle service ran between Central and the ground. The trains were made up of elderly non-corridor coaches hauled variously by 'C13' and 'N5' tanks and 'J10' 0-6-0s. Central itself continued to develop and in 1936 was provided with a 170-ton turntable, converted to vacuum operation in January 1937. By the outbreak of World War 2 it was the largest passenger station on the system, handling an average of 400 trains each day.

The war brought a vast increase in traffic to all parts of the CLC, including Manchester. New sidings were put in at Glazebrook to serve the Lancashire Steel Corporation and the Manchester Ship Canal. At Trafford Park exchange facilities for traffic to and from the trading estate and Ship Canal were similarly enlarged and enhanced. Manchester's rail network also became the target of aerial attack during the winter and summer of 1940-1. The CLC goods warehouse at Central suffered severe damage, with both the roof and top floor being virtually destroyed. The MSJAR

viaduct between Castlefield and Old Trafford Junction was also breached, and it was several months before the line was restored. In the meantime (1 January 1941-22 September 1941), MSJAR services were diverted to Central, using steam trains from Warwick Road (the MSJAR having been electrified in 1931). At Central, glass was removed from the outer platform canopies, and the main arched roof, although still glazed, had an additional covering of tarred hessian, resulting in a gloomy environment for those who continued to use and work in the station. Passenger services were also disrupted with some, such the football specials to Old Trafford, suspended entirely. Others, such as the Liverpool-Manchester express, were reduced to slower running, with the best wartime expresses completing the journey in 53min.

The end of hostilities found Manchester's railway system in a neglected state and a number of schemes were put forward for its improvement. The most far-reaching of these was a plan devised by the City of Manchester in 1945, which proposed that a single new terminus, called Trinity, should replace existing main line stations in the city. Under the scheme, stations such as London Road and Central would have been demolished and the land released for other building projects. The plan came to nothing, although it was apparent that the individual railway companies could not afford to repair the damage caused by six years of emergency working by themselves. The Cheshire Lines fared worse of all, as the parent companies had no spare capital to invest in its reconstruction. As a result, the CLC was unable to return to its prewar condition, although premises in the Manchester area damaged during the Blitz were partially reconditioned and brought back into use.

3

Liverpool

The CLC official *Holiday Guide* for 1927 'From City Streets to Country Lanes' introduces Liverpool as follows:

'The second port of the British Isles and the Gateway to the West is the usual designation of Liverpool. It has been termed the Mecca of the Agent. It is certainly not a manufacturing centre but it is dearly beloved as a transhipment place. It is one of the world's greatest ports and a very fine city.'

Looking back to the early years of the CLC, the importance of Liverpool as a commercial centre during the late 19th century can scarcely be exaggerated. By 1900 over 27% of the total commerce of the Empire was conveyed via Liverpool Docks, as well as the greatest bulk of United States, Canadian, West African and South American passenger traffic. Both types of traffic, worth £173 million a year, were largely handled by railway companies, who served the city with 108 stations. It is against this background that the Cheshire Lines expansion into Liverpool is to be understood and explains why the company chose to locate its headquarters there rather than in Manchester.

The earliest Liverpool section of what became the CLC predated the formation of the Committee. The Garston & Liverpool Railway Act (1861) authorised the GNR and MSLR to construct a railway 3 miles 73 chains in length from Liverpool (Brunswick Docks) to Garston (Dock Road), to connect there with the St Helens Railway (LNWR). Running powers were also granted to the two companies over the LNWR between Garston Dock station and Timperley Junction on the MSJAR, thereby giving a through route to Manchester London Road. In return, the LNWR was granted running powers over sections of the MSLR (to Sheffield) and the GNR (from Peterborough to Grimsby and New Holland). The line opened on 1 June 1864 and was managed by the Liverpool, Garston and Cheshire Railway (GN & MSLR Joint), with Brunswick station, poorly situated to the south of the city, serving as the terminus for both goods and passenger traffic. Additional stations were provided at Mersey Road, Otterspool and St Michaels. The following year a goods station was added at Wavertree (renamed Wavertree & Edge Hill in 1890), connecting with the LNWR main line at Edge Hill but otherwise isolated from the rest of the Joint Line's system.

At this time, much of the traffic from Lancashire and Manchester into Liverpool was carried by the LNWR, who regarded the area as home territory and fiercely contested attempts by rival companies to gain a foothold. Unable to compete on equal terms, the Midland Railway sought an alliance with the GNR and MSLR under the Cheshire Lines Transfer Act of 1865, which transferred several lines (including the Garston & Liverpool Railway) to the newly formed Cheshire Lines Committee and ultimately enabled the Midland to become a full partner. In the meantime, Watkin had put forward a proposal to connect Liverpool with Manchester in the face of severe opposition from the LNWR and LYR. Supported by the GNR and MR, who needed to strengthen their positions in south Lancashire and were concerned by rumours of a merger between the LYR and Great Eastern Railway, the scheme led to the MSLR (Extension to Liverpool) Act 1865, which authorised the construction of a railway from a junction with the MSJAR at Old Trafford to a junction with the Garston & Liverpool Railway in the vicinity of Cressington. It was amended by the MSLR (New Lines) Act 1866, which sanctioned the deviation of the line to a junction with the MSJAR at Cornbrook. The railway was opened in 1873 and vested in the CLC.

Up to 1874 all passenger traffic was dealt with at Brunswick, from where passengers were conveyed by horse-drawn omnibus to the CLC head offices in Alexandra Buildings, James Street. This was clearly an inconvenient arrangement and in 1864 powers were obtained under the Liverpool Central Station Railway Act to build an extension from Brunswick to Ranelagh Street, in the heart of the city. The contract for the extension, which included an intermediate station at St James (closed 1916), went to Kirk & Parry. Despite being only 1¾ miles in length, the new line took 10 years to build, as it was almost entirely in cutting and tunnel and had to be hewn out of red

Above left: The Ranelagh Street frontage of Liverpool Central, shortly before World War 1. Among other detail is the large Lewis's department store beside the station buildings. *David Bownes Collection*

Below left: A 1920s view of Ranelagh Street shows the new Lewis's building, as well as the entrance to the Mersey Railway. *David Bownes Collection*

Above: Liverpool Central concourse before World War 2, showing the steps down to the Mersey Railway's low level station. Other items of interest are; extreme left: one of the clockwork *Rocket* models that used to raise money for the railway homes, the sweet dispensing machines each side of the stairway, and the wall smothered with enamel advertising signs. *British Railways LMR*

sandstone. The rate of construction was also severely handicapped by a clause inserted into the Act by Liverpool Corporation, prohibiting the use of explosives for blasting under the city.

Liverpool Central eventually opened on 2 March 1874, from which time Brunswick ceased to handle passenger traffic. The station had an impressive three-storey façade that served as the new headquarters of the CLC, although departments dealing with claims, fares and season tickets were located in Renshaw Street (later moved to Lawton Street). Inside, the station had seven platforms, five devoted to passengers and two to milk, horses and carriages. However, the tunnelled approach to the station constituted a

bottleneck, made more difficult by a lack of space for sidings at the station itself. Consequently, empties had to back as far as Halewood, but according to contemporary accounts delays were rare, due to the efficiency of the station staff and the responsible officers.

The first stationmaster at Central was George Mason, succeeded in 1900 by Mr S. Denning. He was paid an annual salary of £200 and was responsible for a uniformed staff of 153, together with the 20 or so carters and van boys necessary for the smooth running of a busy Victorian station. In the early years the station under their control put on a daily service of 16 trains in each direction between Liverpool Central and Manchester London Road.

In response to the success of LNWR family omnibuses, which conveyed passengers to and from Lime Street, the CLC purchased three similar vehicles in 1882 at a cost of £90 each, to be worked by contractors based at Central. Oddly, the Officers' Minutes for November 1882 record that these buses were to be 'painted the same colour as those in use by the GN Company in London', possibly as a gesture to the GNR directors who were known to be disgruntled by what they perceived to be the MSLR's domination of the CLC.

Meanwhile, dockland development in north Liverpool had left the CLC in a poor position to exploit seabound traffic. Its only direct connection with the docks was at Brunswick, which was better served by both the LNWR and LYR and which suffered from its southerly location. Nevertheless, Brunswick Goods station underwent a number of improvements during the 1870s and '80s, and was ultimately able to provide facilities for storing up to 20,000 tons of grain, or merchandise of similar bulk, in modern fireproof warehouses. New connections with adjacent docks were completed in 1884 and in particular access was gained to Herculaneum Dock, where a large business in export coal from Lancashire was secured. In connection with this and other improvements, a 40-ton steam crane was installed during the same year to replace the old 25-ton Goliath crane, at a cost of £900.

To compete for a greater share of dockland traffic and to establish a presence in north Liverpool, the CLC purchased 23 acres of land in the Huskisson area. This was a bold strategy, as the area was isolated from the existing CLC system and would require either an expensive low level link from Central or a more circuitous connection skirting the northerly suburbs of the city. In the end, the latter option was chosen and a new line authorised in July 1874 from a junction at Hunt's Cross and Halewood to a junction with the LYR between Aintree and Maghull, together with a line from Fazakerley to Walton-on-the-Hill, which connected (via a short extension) with Huskisson. The contract for what became known locally as the Liverpool North Extension Lines, went to Kirk & Parry and work commenced in 1875. The estimated cost of the extension, which totalled 15 miles, was put at £923,096 but expenses soared as tunnelling and engineering works were required in order to cross major roads and canals. The new line opened on 1 December 1879, with the extension to Husskisson following on 1 July 1880. Intermediate stations were provided at Gateacre, Childwall, Old Swan & Knotty Ash, West Derby and Walton-on-the-Hill. An initial passenger service was put on from Central to Walton (Huskisson opened for passenger traffic on 2 August 1880), although the indirect nature of the route to the city centre, coupled with the fact that it passed through a thinly populated district, meant that most stopping services were terminated at Gateacre. For the same reason, passenger services to and from Huskisson were short lived and withdrawn on 1 May 1885 due to lack of use.

However, it was as an extension for goods traffic that the line was first conceived, and hence it should be judged on that basis. Goods facilities were completed at all stations by 1882, with the main sorting sidings located at Walton and Halewood, and a new engine shed erected at Allerton (opened 1882). Additional goods lines were laid between Hunt's Cross West Junction and Halewood East Junction in 1883. At Huskisson, a vast complex of warehouses and sidings was constructed at a final cost of £150,000 (1883 figure). This included a passenger station, stablings, sidings, cattle pens sufficient to permit 2,000 head of cattle, cotton and grain wharfs, offices, a water tank, a turntable and a small timber yard in Victoria Road. At Foster Street, adjacent to Huskisson, the CLC established lairage capable of accommodating a further 1,200 cattle to cope with the very large traffic in Irish cattle which the station dealt with each week. Indeed, in 1898 the *Railway Magazine* claimed that the accommodation for livestock provided at Huskisson was unsurpassed anywhere in Britain. Cattle traffic was also important at Old Swan & Knotty Ash, which was renamed Knotty Ash & Stanley in 1888 to advertise its closeness to Stanley Cattle Market.

The North Liverpool Lines were equally important for their connections with other railway systems. The connection at Aintree with the East Lancashire section of the LYR opened a new route for Midland traffic from the north to Huskisson. Similarly, Fazakerley Junction provided a connection with the Langton Dock Branch of the MR, which came into operation in June 1885. The CLC was also able to serve the growing number of factories in the Walton/Halewood areas, the best known being those of Hartley's Jam (1886) and Jacob's Biscuits (1913).

Additional schemes for extending the CLC's dock frontage were put forward in 1875 and 1892, when the Company purchased the Jericho and Otterspool estates, situated mid-distance between Herculaneum and Garston Docks, at a total cost of £121,750. The two estates gave a continuous river frontage of 1,120yd, but plans for their development by the CLC were eventually dropped and the land was sold to Liverpool Corporation in 1925.

Throughout the late 19th century repeated attempts were made to provide a direct link between Huskisson and Central. In 1888 the MSLR obtained powers to construct an underground route but this proposal was blocked by the Midland and Great Northern directors, who felt they had expended enough capital on the Joint Company and wished to make a stand against Watkin's continual schemes for the enlargement of the CLC. Thus, a great opportunity to provide Liverpool with a circular railway was lost, while the North Liverpool Lines, and later the Southport Extension, suffered due to their roundabout route into Liverpool Central.

Similarly, Watkin's plans for a connection with the Mersey Railway via Central station were only partly successful, due to opposition from his partners in the CLC. Watkin had hoped that such a connection would give the CLC direct access to Birkenhead and the various goods depots clustered on the opposite banks of the Mersey. As it was, these could only be reached via Helsby and the Birkenhead Joint Line. Instead, a low level link was made at Central with the Mersey Railway for passengers only and opened on 11 January 1892. The new underground station served as the terminus of the Mersey Railway, handling an incredible 740 passenger trains a day.

Services at Central also witnessed a rapid expansion during this period. As the terminus of four companies (CLC, MSLR, GNR and MR) the station had direct access to over 3,000 track miles, which was claimed by the CLC as a figure reached by few railway companies in Britain operating from a single terminus. Of course, to the passenger it was simply one station offering a wide range of services, and by the early 1900s there were 170 trains a day using Central. Apart from local (CLC) services, the GCR ran through trains to Sheffield, the eastern counties, Hull (especially for European emigrants crossing England en route to America) and Grimsby (for services to Rotterdam and the Continent). The Midland Railway offered trains to Cromer via Leicester and the Saxby and Bourne line on the M&GN Joint, together with through services to Sheffield (via Chinley), Matlock, Nottingham, Birmingham, Bristol and London. Typically, the GNR gained less than its partners from the expansion of the CLC and ran one through train a day to King's Cross, which fared badly compared to the much quicker and shorter route offered by the LNWR to Euston from Liverpool Lime Street. Other companies operating out of Central included the Great Eastern Railway, which put on a cross-country service to Cromer and Lowestoft, and the North Eastern Railway, which ran regular 'emigrant specials' to Hull (via Godley). In addition, the station handled a large volume of excursion traffic from all parts of Britain — the average number of Bank Holiday Specials for 1900 being 40.

However, as we have seen, the jewel in the crown of the CLC's timetable was the hourly express between Liverpool and Manchester, which had a fastest journey time of only 40min. From Manchester, a wide range of destinations was available to the Liverpool traveller, including the Cheshire section of the CLC.

Another source of revenue for the CLC was from holidaymakers and passengers travelling to the Isle of Man and Ireland, who were conveyed free of charge in horse drawn omnibuses from Central station to the landing stage. The CLC was the first railway company to offer this service and its investment paid off well. By the late 1890s, the majority of passengers departing from Liverpool for Dublin and Belfast arrived from inland towns via the CLC system. Moreover, the introduction of fast passenger steamers, such as *Empress Queen* and *Mona's Isle*, by the Isle of Man Steam Packet Co, dramatically reduced crossing times and enabled the CLC to offer day returns to Man from as far afield as Southport and Manchester. The cost of first and saloon class travel to either Douglas or Ramsey from Manchester Central in 1910 was 18s, or 10s 6d for third class and steerage.

During the summer months the CLC ran trains connecting with the sailings of the Liverpool & North Wales Steamship Co (LNWSSC), which offered regular excursions to Llandudno, Bangor, Beaumaris and Menai Bridge, and sea cruises round the Isle of Anglesey. A favourite for this services was the LNWSSC's paddle steamer *St Tudno*, which was used extensively to illustrate CLC holiday guides and timetables. To attract holidaymakers, passengers' luggage could be collected and delivered in advance to Liverpool Central from homes or hotels near to CLC stations. In 1910 the cost of this service was one shilling per package, with 1s 6d charged for luggage carried across Liverpool to meet the steamers. The service proved extremely popular and during the 1890s and 1900s the Cheshire Lines purchased a number of covered luggage vans to cope with the increased demand. Short break holidays, advertised as 'Circular Tours', were also offered during the summer months from any CLC station to Dublin, Belfast and North Wales via Liverpool and the Isle of Man. Thus, depending on the type of tour chosen, holidaymakers could leave from their home station, travel to Liverpool Central, join a steamer to the Isle of Man, continue their journey to Ireland at their leisure and return home along the North Wales coast, stopping off at resorts such as Llandudno.

Away from the docks, the CLC's original development in south Liverpool had resulted in an enormous growth of suburban passenger traffic. Garston, Cressington, Mersey Road and Otterspool were acknowledged as being among the most attractive residential districts of the city, and the CLC put on a frequent service between these stations and Central. Mersey Road also benefited from its proximity to Aigburth cricket ground and a large number of specials were run during match times.

Similarly in north and east Liverpool, West Derby, Knotty Ash, Childwall and Gateacre

Left: Liverpool Central's signalbox was squeezed into a confined space at the platform ends, just before the lines plunged into the approach tunnel. Though the box had common features with other CLC signalboxes, the unusual wide overhang of the roof can be seen here; photographed on 29 September 1966.
Roger Golder

Left: The exit from Brunswick Depot in the early 1950s. 'Director' No 62658 *Prince George* is receiving running gear attention under the sheer-legs while 'J11' No 64304 runs off shed. The 'Directors' were still the line's top-link power at the time. Brunswick suffered by being squeezed into a very limited available space.
Rev A. W. V. Mace/Milepost 92½

Above right: 'X4' Single No 967 passes through Halewood with a Manchester-Liverpool express, *c*1913. The ringed signal arm controlled access to the yard.
H. Gordon Tidey/ Brian Stephenson Collection

Right: Two pages from the CLC 1901 official guide, advertising its own excursion services and the sightseeing potential of the Liverpool Overhead Railway. One curiosity is that Beaumaris never had a station.
Author's Collection

developed reputations for being the favoured suburbs of Liverpool merchants. World War 1 brought further traffic to the area, as a reception camp for American troops was set up near Knotty Ash, resulting in increased use of the station and its facilities. However, Walton-on-the-Hill was less successful and closed for passengers from 1 January 1918, but remained in occasional use for excursion traffic into the 1930s. During the 1920s, new council estates in north Liverpool resulted in additional CLC stations being built at Clubmoor (14 April 1927) and Warbreck (1 August 1929), although changes in population saw Childwall close on 1 January 1931 due to lack of traffic.

No account of the CLC's presence in Liverpool would be complete without mention of the substantial horse racing traffic handled at Aintree.

First named Aintree Racecourse, the station opened on race days only from 13 July 1880, and was only put into regular use following the opening of the Southport Extension (1 September 1884), when its name was shortened to Aintree. Two rival stations on the LYR competed for the valuable Grand National traffic but Aintree CLC was by far the largest of the three, with five passenger platforms and a sixth for horses. To give some idea of the traffic involved, a contemporary account published in the *Railway Magazine* (1935) commented:

'On Grand National day the sidings, locomotive depots and stations are worked to the limits of their capacity in dealing with the enormous number of special and ordinary trains arriving from near and far.'

Cheshire Lines.

☞ THE FAVOURITE ROUTE

FROM

Lancashire and Cheshire
to the North Wales Coast

IS

Via LIVERPOOL.

CHEAP EXCURSION TICKETS are issued for Half-Day, One Day, Week End, 10 or 11 Days, and for longer periods.

The Tickets are issued DAILY, Sundays included, at the undermentioned Stations.

Manchester (C), Chorlton-c-Hardy, Urmston, Flixton, Irlam, Cadishead, Glazebrook, *Padgate, Warrington, Sankey, *Farnworth, *Hough Green, Northwich, *Knutsford, *Mobberley,	*Peel Causeway, *Altrincham, *Timperley, *Brooklands, *Sale, Stretford, *Old Trafford, *Godley, *Woodley, Stockport (Tiviot Dale), *Baguley, *West Timperley, *Southport (Lord St.) & *Birkdale.	TO LLANDUDNO, BANGOR, BEAUMARIS, AND MENAI BRIDGE.

*—No Bookings from these Stations on Sundays.

Popular Afternoon Trips to Llandudno
ON SATURDAYS & SUNDAYS
During the Summer Months.

For Fares, Train Service & full particulars, see Programmes issued, to be obtained Free at Cheshire Lines Stations, or from the undersigned.

Central Station, Liverpool. **DAVID MELDRUM, Manager.**

Punctual Service of Trains every 5 minutes.

Splendid View of six miles of Docks and River Frontage.

Quickest Route to all the Docks, Seaforth, Waterloo, and Great Crosby; also Prince's and Sefton Parks.

LIVERPOOL OVERHEAD Electric RAILWAY

MOVING STAIRCASE

SEAFORTH SANDS STATION.

SPECIAL RATES to Large Parties of Excursionists.

RAILWAY FARES—
1st Class 3d.   2nd Class 2d.
FOR ANY DISTANCE.

3, James Street, Liverpool. **S. B. COTTRELL, General Manager.**

Table **235**

A thin line between the hour and minute figures indicates p.m.

Table 235 — CHESHIRE LINES STATIONS, via MANCHESTER (Central) and via STOCKPORT (Tiviot Dale).

SUNDAYS.

WEEK DAYS.

Stations (read downward):

London (St. P.) dep.
Leicester
Nottingham
Derby
Burton
Sheffield
Chinley
*Stockport (T.D.) arr.
Cheadle
Northenden
Baguley
West Timperley
Partington
Cadishead
*Manchester (Central) arr.
Trafford Park
Urmston
Chassen Road
Flixton
Irlam
Glazebrook
St. Helens (Cen.)
Wigan (Central)
Padgate
Sankey (for Penk'th)
Warrington
Tanhouse Lane
Widnes (Central)
Farnworth
Hough Gn. (for Ditton)
Halewood
Gateacre arr.
Knotty Ash & Stanley
West Derby
Aintree
Airedale (Beach)
Birkdale (Palace)
Southport (L. St.)
Hunt's Cross arr.
Garston
Cressington & Grassendale
Mersey Road
Otterspool
St. Michael's
Liverpool (Central) arr.

Notes:
A—Leicester 7.20, Nottingham 7.5, Derby 8.6 a.m. on Saturdays.
B—Four minutes later on Saturdays.
C—Saturdays only.
D—Arrive Glazebrook 8.9 p.m. on Saturdays.
E—Arrive Glazebrook and Ambergale, 7.5 a.m. on Saturdays via Derby.
F—Via Butterley and Ambergale.
H—Saturdays excepted, change at Warrington and Halewood.
J—Change at Hunt's Cross. One class only.
L—Change at Hunt's Cross.
6.45 p.m. on Saturdays only except on Saturdays.
M—Gateacre 12.1, Knotty Ash 12.10, West Derby 12.13, Aintree 12.23, Airedale Beach 12.48, Southport
N—Via Butterley 12.6, and Southport 12.58 p.m. on Saturdays.
N—3.15 p.m. on Saturday via Manchester (C.).

SX—Saturdays excepted.

R—Saturdays excepted. One class only.
S—Saturdays only.
T—One class only on Saturdays.
U—Arrive Glazebrook 8.9 p.m. on Saturdays.
V—Change at Warrington.
W—Change at Warrington and Hunt's Cross.
o—One class only.
o—8.24 p.m. on Saturdays.
k—Twelve minutes earlier on Saturdays.
k—Three minutes later on Saturdays.

m—Change at Hunt's Cross.
n—Arrive nine minutes later on Saturdays.
q—On Saturdays, Gateacre 1.14, Aintree 1.25, Airedale
Beach 1.45, and Southport 1.53 p.m.
r—Arrive Creesington 4.51 p.m. on Saturdays.
t—10.28 a.m. on Saturdays until October 21st (inclusive).
u—Manchester (Cen.) 6.24 p.m. on Saturdays (6.33 p.m. on December 23rd).
v—4.59 p.m. on Saturdays.
T—Via Gateacre.

Above: An extract from the LMS winter 1939/40 timetable proof, showing the service part of the Cheshire Lines. This timetable was never introduced or published, as the outbreak of war led to a reduced emergency timetable being operated.
Author's Collection

B 2633
CHESHIRE LINES
Liverpool Cen. 2
PARCEL STAMP 7/-
PAID
No. of Packages.

B 2632
CHESHIRE LINES
Liverpool Cen. 2
PARCEL STAMP 7/-
PAID
No. of Packages.

Right: Liverpool was not just a port for freight and great liners; many short-haul packet routes, including some concentrating on the pleasure cruise market, served there too. From 1891 to 1963 the Liverpool & North Wales Steamship Co's ships sailed along the coast to Llandudno pier and beyond to Anglesey. They were popular for days out, short cruises and, of course, as a different way to get to and from your holiday resort. The CLC naturally allied itself to this potential market and advertised its services to meet the North Wales steamers at Liverpool. The SS *St Seiriol* is seen passing Great Ormes Head on the run from Llandudno to Anglesey in 1935.
Ken Saunders Collection

Lower right: The *St Seiriol* passes through the Menai Strait and under Telford's great suspension bridge; this was a popular trip for many years and the CLC made sure that it conveyed as many intending passengers as possible to Liverpool.
Ken Saunders Collection

During the 1930s, the CLC ran an average of six additional express trains from Manchester to Aintree on Grand National day, with further specials from Southport and Liverpool. The LMS and LNER also ran a large number of specials to Aintree CLC from all parts of their systems. Once unloaded, the engines stabled their carriages and waited near the station until all the specials had arrived, before proceeding, coupled in twos and threes, to Walton-on-the-Hill shed. In addition, two of the LNER engines, those of the double-headed Bridlington special, regularly used Southport turntable 14½ miles north of Aintree. Other logistical problems were encountered due to the length of special trains. For example, the LNER King's Cross Pullman (inaugurated in 1928 and always Pacific-hauled) was required to make a double stop at Aintree to put down passengers. In total, it was estimated that an average of 6,000 passengers used Aintree CLC on Grand National day during the 1930s, which although less than the combined 24,000 who used the two LMS stations, still required considerable planning and increased staffing levels.

With the outbreak of World War 2, parts of the CLC's Liverpool system saw an increase in traffic of over 200%, while the city itself became the focus of sustained aerial attacks. Liverpool Central was hit by enemy action and dock traffic was severely disrupted, with Brunswick Docks being temporarily the only point from which traffic could be accepted from all railway companies to and from the south docks area. Huskisson Goods station was also seriously damaged by bombs and virtually destroyed during a raid in 1941. At the same time, the whole of the undercover facilities for handling sundries were demolished, and sections of the station were flooded following a direct hit on the nearby Leeds & Liverpool Canal.

To cope with the greatly increased volume of goods traffic, additional sidings were laid at Halewood and Walton in 1941, and some passenger services were withdrawn. The CLC continued to operate even during the worst of the disruption, but it was not until after nationalisation in 1948 that all of the damage was repaired and the Liverpool lines returned to their prewar condition.

4

Chester

Chester stands on the site of Deva Castra, built by the Romans in AD79 and the largest known fortress in Britain. Trade routes to Ireland later made Chester the most prosperous port in the Northwest, a status which it recovered after the English Civil War. However, by the middle of the 18th century silting of the river had forced the Irish trade to Parkgate, nearer the mouth of the Dee, and then to Liverpool. The position improved again with the Industrial Revolution, when canal and railway networks made Chester an important regional trading centre.

A two-mile ring of medieval and Roman wall encircles a centre of Tudor and Victorian buildings. Among the ancient streets are the Rows — two tiers of half-timbered, galleried medieval shops — and a cathedral dating mainly from the 14th century. The Roodee, which lies between the western wall of the city and the river, has been the site of Chester races since 1540. Boating on the placid Dee appealed to the well-to-do of south Lancashire and Cheshire. All these features combined to make the county town of Cheshire an important tourist centre. To trade and tourism add the fact that Chester is the gateway to North Wales and it became a natural objective for the expanding Cheshire Lines.

Powers to build a railway from Mouldsworth (CLC) to Chester were granted under the Chester & West Cheshire Junction Railway Act, 5 July 1865 (MSLR & GNR Joint), which was absorbed by the CLC on 10 August 1866, prior to the opening of the line. After much negotiation, the

Below: Chester Northgate was the least grand of the CLC's main termini. It is seen here in its latter years, looking down-at-heel and with much of the train shed glass missing — and little sign of life. Posters advertise cheap tickets to the North Wales coast and other destinations. *John E. Field*

contract for the work went to Knight & Rose and construction was finally put in hand during 1871. The railway ran from Mouldsworth Junction to Chester Northgate and necessitated the purchase of 11 acres of land at Chester from Lord Kilmorey, including Northgate House which was demolished. The total length of the extension was 7 miles 43 chains of double line, with eight overbridges and 15 underbridges, the steepest gradient being 1 in 72. Intermediate stations were at Tarvin & Barrow (renamed Barrow for Tarvin in 1883) and Mickle Trafford — both of which served small rural communities.

The extension was opened for goods traffic on 2 November 1874 and for passengers on 1 May 1875, having cost over £225,000 to build. At Chester there were separate goods facilities and a two-road engine shed, which was originally a sub-shed of Northwich. Although unprepossessing externally, the passenger station was provided with two platforms with four lines between (two for standage), surmounted by an overall roof. At this time the CLC put on a daily service of five trains in each direction between Manchester Oxford Road (MSJAR) and Chester Northgate.

The potential of the Chester & West Cheshire Junction Railway to provide a connection was keenly felt by the parent companies. A junction was laid to join the Birkenhead Joint Railway at Mickle Trafford, which should have come into operation on 1 March 1875, but as the companies involved could not agree about its use it was never connected, and was finally removed in 1903. A new junction was put in at Mickle Trafford at government expense during World War 2 — the object being to make greater use of the route into Birkenhead via Chester (CLC) and Bidston (LNER) and so relieve the other lines serving the docks. It was opened on 4 October 1942 and intended as a wartime measure only.

Sir Edward Watkin, saw the newly opened line as a means to expand the MSLR into North Wales and the Wirral. This he achieved with the opening of the Chester and Hawarden section of the MSLR (March 1890), which connected with the Wrexham, Mold & Connah's Quay Railway (an MSLR subsidiary, absorbed by the GCR in 1904), and later with the Hawarden-Bidston line (known as the North Wales & Liverpool Railway), which opened in 1896 and connected with the Wirral Railway.

Despite building its own station in Chester (Liverpool Road), MSLR services for North Wales usually departed from Northgate, from where connections could be made with the MSLR main line at Manchester. For this privilege the MSLR credited the CLC with a one-mile proportion and terminals on all goods and passenger traffic

Above: Signals at the platform ends of Northgate in 1953. *R. F. Roberts/Author's Collection*

arising or terminating at Chester Northgate. In addition, the MSLR paid the CLC £50 per year to cover the use of Chester Goods station and a rental of £24 for each engine stabled in the Cheshire Lines shed at Chester, with a further 6d being charged for the use of the turntable. The MSLR also paid a proportion of the charges towards maintenance and working costs of Chester East and South Junction signal cabins. Even so, there can be little doubt that the MSLR enjoyed considerable benefit from the CLC's extension to Chester, and there is evidence that both the Great Northern and Midland directors felt aggrieved by this.

At Wrexham there was a connection with a Cambrian Railway subsidiary, the Wrexham & Ellesmere Railway, which from 1896 enabled the CLC to run through trains to West Wales via Northgate and Wrexham. In his interview with the *Railway Magazine* in 1899, David Meldrum was able to boast that the cordial relations which existed between his company and the Cambrian had resulted in the inauguration of popular summer expresses from Manchester to Aberystwyth and Barmouth, for which special carriages had been built.

At the time of opening, Chester Northgate employed 20 permanent staff, in addition to several 'boys', carters and guards based at the

Left: 'J39' 0-6-0 No 64743 heads a goods train along the Chester line through Delamere Forest in 1957. *Peter Norton/ Author's Collection*

Below left: Chester Liverpool Road was the MSLR station in the city. It had long been closed to all traffic when No 64743 rumbled through on a mineral train for Dee Marsh Junction sidings on 17 September 1954. *R. J. Morris*

Right: Staff line up for a group portrait in happier days at Northgate, probably around the time of the Grouping. CLC cap badges are much in evidence and almost every adult sports a moustache.
David Bownes Collection

station. The highest paid of these was the station master, who also acted as the goods agent, receiving £2 2s per week, which was about the same as his counterparts at the larger CLC stations, such as Northwich and Stockport, but considerably more than the £1 5s average paid to station masters at less busy places. At the other end of the scale were the lad porters, porters and carriage washers, who were paid between 14 and 18 shillings a week, depending on their length of service.

Goods traffic at Chester was extremely varied, reflecting both the importance of the city as a business centre, and the CLC's link with the coalfields of North Wales and the industrial area of Flintshire reached via the MSLR. By 1884 the station was handling an average of 1,500 tons per month, compared with only 775 tons during 1875. In 1903 facilities at Chester Goods station were enlarged at a cost of £225, as traffic had increased by over 123% during the preceding 10

years, largely due to the use made of it by the GCR. This growth continued into the 20th century, with the emergence of new clients, such as the steel works of Sumners & Sons in Hawarden.

Chester was an important tourist destination, and the Cheshire Lines did all it could to promote the ancient attractions of the city. 'Tourist Tickets' to Chester Northgate, via Manchester Central, were offered to the holidaymaker by each of the parent companies, with breaks in the journey allowed at 'the old world town of Knutsford', Delamere ('for Hatchmere Lake and the Forest'), and Mouldsworth ('for the Liverpool and Manchester Sanatoriums and the Forest'). In 1910 the cost of such a ticket from Nottingham was 23s 6d first class and 13s second class, while from Manchester the traveller would have paid 9s 6d and 5s respectively.

The Cheshire Lines held its own with the large railways in public relations, promotion and

publicity, as it did in so many other aspects of railway management. It could encourage flowery prose with the best of them and W. Hartley Bracewell, writing in the *Railway Magazine* in 1899, gave the following description of travelling by train to Chester.

'Both Liverpool and Manchester are within easy reach, and each route is taken through undeniably charming scenery, so that while passengers profit by the short swift run, they have the benefit of a landscaped view — a panorama of hill and dale — such as Ruskin would revel in painting with his versatile pen. Waving cornfields relieve at intervals the verdancy of broad pasture lands on which horses and cattle browse at ease. Here we get a peep at a red-tiled ivy-grown cottage screened in a bush of willows, with a garden hemmed by a stout hedge of hawthorn. A rustic seat overhung with elderberry and the trembling Aspen, is passed by in a meadow through which a path winds in to an inviting wood. There across the fields a sun-burnt son of the soil is hard at work with the plough, and at a point where the road runs for a short distance parallel with the metals a trusty old grey mare jogs along in the shafts of a "rickety rackety" milk cart, driven by a rubicund, contented-looking farmer, whose headgear impresses one as having lost its youth years ago. But youth we do see, and in its purest phase, for if not in a hat, it is presented in the shape of a comely little milkmaid, wearing a light blue frock and pink sunbonnet, crossing a neighbouring farmyard. She raises her head as we dash by, and affords us just one glimpse of a type of country beauty, lovelier, I think as I see it, in its innocence and simplicity, than all the fascinating physiognomies that London ever produced. Thus from the windows of those comfortably upholstered spring-seated carriages, the vibration of which is practically nil, we witness an ever changing picture. We see all that I have noted and much more and have scarcely remarked upon the splendour of an undulation that stretches far away into the recesses of mountainous Wales, than our journey is at an end, and we step out to find ourselves in one of the historic haunts where antiquarians congregate.'

Another significant source of revenue was traffic connected with the famous race meetings held on the Roodee. To cope with the increased passenger numbers on race days, special express trains of 15 coaches each were laid on between Manchester and Chester, covering the 40-mile distance in 55min. Because of the length of these trains, the CLC was obliged to extend the arrival and departure platforms in 1905 at a cost of £540, and again in 1911 when the departure platform was lengthened by a further 47yd to accommodate outward traffic during race times.

POST CARD.

THE ADDRESS ONLY TO be WRITTEN HERE.

Cheshire Lines.

Manager's Office,
Liverpool,
19.........

Dear Sir,
I am in receipt of your letter of
the ....
which shall have my immediate attention.

Yours truly,
DAVID MELDRUM.

ECCLESTON FERRY, RIVER DEE, CHESTER.

Cheshire Lines Railway. CHESTER is an ancient and venerable city, and will well repay a gate Station is situated close to the numerous attractions of the C

Goods trains were prohibited from working the line during peak periods on race days, and the CLC drafted in extra staff and police from nearby stations to ensure the smooth running of passenger traffic. In this the CLC was particularly successful and managed to attract the lion's share of race goers, to the detriment of Chester General station (GW&LNW Joint) — a circumstance helped no doubt by the proximity of Northgate to the racecourse, which, as the *Railway Magazine* sniffily pointed out in 1913, was, 'in itself sufficient to secure the patronage of much of the motley crowd which follows so faithfully the fixtures made . . . for the furtherance of the sport of kings'.

In terms of ordinary passenger traffic, the CLC's main service from Chester Northgate was to Manchester Central via Altrincham, Knutsford and Northwich. By the eve of World War 1, the CLC was running 10 passenger trains a day in each direction between the two cities — a figure which remained more or less constant for the remainder of the company's existence. The mean average for stopping trains on this route during

the 1930s was 1hr 33min, although in the pre-Grouping era the journey had taken up to 20min longer, due to delays at Altrincham, Northwich and Cuddington to meet connecting services. In 1932 the cost of a return ticket was 14s 6d first class, and 8s 8d for third class travel.

However, from the 1890s the majority of trains leaving Chester Northgate were MSLR (later GCR/LNER) in origin. By 1910 the GCR were running up to 15 passenger trains a day between Chester and Wrexham, Shotton and Hawarden, with additional trains on Saturdays. As already noted, these services provided connections with other companies and offered through services to Bidston, Seacombe and Liverpool. The LNER made similar use of Chester Northgate, offering frequent trains to Shotton and Wrexham. In contrast, appearances of Midland, Great Northern and, latterly, LMS coaching stock at Northgate were limited to the occasional excursion train, thus highlighting the original motives of Watkin and the rewards which the Chester & West Cheshire Junction Railway brought to his company.

5

Southport

Modelled on the exclusive resorts of the South of France and laid out as a garden city, Southport became known in publicity material as the 'Montpellier of the North'. A fashionable watering place and residential area for the businessmen of Manchester and Liverpool, it was closely linked in spirit with the main CLC network. It thus represented an appropriate final destination for the company at the end of its expansionist phase.

A scheme for an extension to Southport was first put before the Committee in 1878, when it resolved to support the Bill and work the railway, but not to subscribe to the capital. However, the Midland and Great Northern directors refused to concur with Watkin's proposal that the CLC should lease the line. Three years later, the Bill for a railway from a junction near Aintreee CLC to Southport passed the Commons Committee, but landowners' opposition resulted in the Lords cutting back the extension to a terminus at

Birkdale (enacted on 11 August 1881). In the next session the company was more successful and on 18 August 1882 Parliamentary sanction was granted to continue the line into Southport, on the understanding that the railway would build and lay out a park for the townspeople.

Watkin's enthusiasm for CLC involvement with the Southport company was never shared by his partners, who argued that the town was already well served by the LYR, East Lancashire Railway

Below: The concourse of Southport Lord Street on 29 July 1951. Though it gives a good idea of this pleasing terminus, the lack of passengers in the middle of summer is significant. Standing at platform 3 is '4F' 0-6-0 No 44285, which must raise questions about the standard of service offered compared to the ex-L&Y station across the town. *Stan Garth/ P. Ward Collection*

Above: The station throat on the same day, showing the platforms that had been lengthened for interwar excursion traffic. The station clock tower stands beyond the overall roof. Despite being close to the centre of Southport, the station has an air of desolation about it. Both it and the line were to finish in less than six months' time, in the days when things had to be really bad for a railway to close! *Stan Garth*

Left: Southport claimed for Lord Street the title of one of England's most fashionable shopping streets. This Edwardian view looks along it towards the station — the clock tower is in the background — in the days before motor traffic made it hazardous for pedestrians to stroll off the pavements. *Author's Collection*

and West Lancashire Railway. However, as always, Watkin had his eyes on a more ambitious prize — a direct route for the MSLR from Manchester to Blackpool. He proposed to do this by using the Southport Extension as a vehicle to connect with the WLR main line to Preston, from where access to Blackpool could be achieved by the construction of a nominally independent railway under MSLR control. During the early 1870s Watkin had even entered into negotiations regarding the possible lease of the WLR by the MSLR, and over the next decade he put forward a variety of schemes to further his goal of reaching Blackpool, including the proposed extension of the MSLR Wigan Branch to join the WLR at Longton,

near Preston. In this Watkin proved unsuccessful but in the process his intrigues had firmly tied the Southport company with the CLC.

Construction of the extension, which totalled 14 miles 3 chains, was rapid and the CLC hoped to start working the line on 31 December 1883. However, the opening was delayed as the railway failed to pass inspection, owing to the inadequacy of the permanent way. Moreover, the Extension Company had run out of money and was initially unable to provide accommodation for either staff or goods. As a result, when passenger services finally commenced on 1 September 1884 they were forced to run at reduced speed until the line was put in good order, while the provision of goods facilities was not completed until April 1886.

The Southport terminus occupied a prime site on Lord Street, one of the smartest shopping areas in the north of England. It stood adjacent to the Winter Gardens and consisted of two side platforms with a central island. Separate goods facilities and a two-road engine shed were also provided. Intermediate stations were at Birkdale Palace, Woodville and Ainsdale (renamed Woodvale 1898), Barton & Halsall (renamed Mossbridge 1894), Altcar and Hillhouse, Lydiate, and Sefton (renamed Sefton & Maghull 1886).

In addition, Aintree opened for regular use, whereas previously it had opened only during race times. In the early years, rolling stock and coaches were supplied by the parent companies, and a service of eight trains a day between Southport and Manchester and nine between Southport and Liverpool, with additional trains to Gateacre and Warrington, was provided. From 1885 the Midland ran a Pullman Express to St Pancras, which did the journey in five hours, twice daily Monday to Saturday and once on Sunday.

The only junction on the extension was with the Liverpool, Southport & Preston Junction Railway (LSPJR) at Hillhouse, which came into operation on 1 October 1887. In return for an annual user charge paid to the CLC, the LSPJR ran a daily service of 22 passenger trains between Southport Central on the WLR and Aintree via Hillhouse Junction and Altcar. The service was later cut back to Barton at the end of the LSPJR line from Southport, with only some trains going through to connect with the Cheshire Lines at Altcar. Opinions differ as to why this service became known as the Altcar Bob. Whether it was because the original fare from Southport to Altcar was a shilling or whether it was since one of the early drivers had been called Bob, or even, the most likely, because 'Bob' was a popular name for small engines and for many years the service was operated by an LYR rail motor, is not now known. However, whatever the reason, the name is charming and has entered into Lancashire railway legend. Under an Act of 1897 the LSPJR and the WLR were absorbed by the Lancashire & Yorkshire Railway, which thus obtained running powers over the Southport and Cheshire Lines Extension Railway to Aintree. In consideration of the CLC not opposing the Bill, the LYR agreed to guarantee a minimum payment of £1,500 per year to the Extension Co in respect of this traffic.

At the time of opening (1884), Southport Lord Street employed 33 staff, including the station master, several clerks, six passenger guards, four porters, four carriage cleaners, three lampmen,

four signalmen, two shunters, one van man and van boy, a station cleaner and a policeman. The next largest station was Birkdale Palace, which employed 10 staff, while the other six stations on the Extension, including Aintree, were each staffed by either four or five railwaymen. All staff were employees of the Cheshire Lines, rather than the Extension Company, and as such wore standard CLC uniforms.

From the start things did not go well for the Southport company. The competition identified by the Midland and Great Northern directors proved to be well founded. Unable to attract sufficient customers, the Southport directors were obliged to call in an official receiver towards the end of 1888, as the company was no longer in a position to pay its debenture shareholders. At this point, the CLC's parent companies stepped in to prevent outright bankruptcy and the possible closure of the line.

It was agreed that the extension would be worked by the CLC in perpetuity but retain its own identity. This was confirmed under the Southport & Cheshire Lines Extension Railway Act (1889) which pledged the CLC to guarantee

debenture stock at 3% per annum on capital of £200,000, on condition that the CLC received 60% of gross receipts up to £20 per mile per week and 55% in respect of gross receipts thereafter, the Extension Company being credited with the remainder. In the event of receipts being less than £6,000 the CLC was to make up such a sum, the average earning of the extension being then about £7,000 per year. Under Section 76 of the Railways Act 1921 the Committee guaranteed to the SCLER a traffic revenue on the basis of rates, fares, tolls, etc which had been operative in 1913.

A result of this arrangement was the introduction of express passenger trains to Liverpool and Manchester, making it possible for commuters to work in these cities and live in Southport. The CLC was anxious to encourage this traffic and in April 1892 responded to a memorial from the residents of Southport for additional fast trains to Manchester during the morning and afternoon rush hours. By 1913 the fastest of these completed the journey from Lord Street to Manchester Central in 1hr 2min, stopping only at Birkdale and West Derby. The more usual time for stopping trains on this route was 2hr. Similar expresses were offered to Liverpool, although again the majority of trains provided a local service, with an average journey time of 1hr 23min. In 1910 the cost of a season ticket between these two destinations was £18, while from Southport to Manchester it was £27 8s. Alternatively, a first class season ticket could be purchased from Southport to both Liverpool and Manchester for £32 10s. Equally important, in terms of daily revenue, were the frequent stopping trains from Southport to Gateacre and Hunt's Cross, from where connections could be made to Warrington and other parts of the CLC system.

From 1 January 1917, all stations on the extension were closed to passenger traffic for the remaining duration of the war. With the exception of Mossbridge, they reopened to passengers in part for the Aintree races of March 1919, and were completely restored to passenger use on 1 April 1919.

In contrast, goods traffic played a far less significant role in the life of the SCLER. Southport had been the first of the stations on the extension to open for this traffic in June 1885, when nine additional staff were taken on to work the new goods facility. The station also ran a delivery service and kept three horses and four 'lurries' (later increased) for this purpose. However, for most of the line's existence there were only two goods trains a day in each direction between Southport and either Walton or Halewood sidings. Only one of these stopped at the intermediate stations on the extension 'when required for traffic purposes', although a far greater volume of foreign goods trains passed over the southernmost section of the line via Hillhouse Junction.

However, perhaps the most important traffic on the Southport Extension was from tourism. Advertised by the CLC as 'Sunny Southport', the town owed a great deal to its reputation as a

fashionable health resort, and between 1871 and 1891 its population rose from 18,000 to 46,000. The most noticeable area of expansion was towards Ainsdale, and as the SCLER ran along the coast at this point it was hoped that it would benefit from the development. Consequently, a new passenger station was opened on 19 June 1901 between Birkdale Palace and Woodvale, called Seaside (renamed Ainsdale Beach in 1912). During the summer months the CLC ran large numbers of excursion trains to Southport from starting points such as Liverpool, Manchester, Warrington, Buxton, Matlock, Sheffield, Worksop, Nottingham, Leicester, Lincoln and London. All classes of passenger were provided for and special invalid saloon, family and through carriages were made available to the holidaymaker. In 1898 it was estimated that Lord Street alone handled over 40,000 passengers during the summer bank holidays. Among the many attractions offered by the town were the popular Marine Lakes, the Winter Gardens and the famous pier, which for many years were used to illustrate the cover of CLC public timetables.

Of all the excursions run to Southport, such as those to the annual August bank holiday Floral Féte (in later years known as the Southport Flower Show), one event calls for special mention. This was the total eclipse of the sun which took place on 29 June 1927. It was the first total eclipse since 1724 and generated an enormous amount of excitement from the press and public alike. The 'totality' band stretched from North Wales across to Hartlepool and Middlesbrough, with Southport, positioned in the centre of the band, regarded as one of the best places to see it. The eclipse was vigorously marketed by both the CLC and LMS, who ran unprecedented numbers of excursion trains to Southport from all parts of England and Wales.

As we have seen, despite the volume of tourist and commuter traffic, the Southport Extension was not as successful as its promoters had hoped and was unable to compete with the LYR (later LMS) main lines from Southport to Manchester and Liverpool once the Allerton line was opened. Before this, the LYR ran via Bolton and the CLC was actually faster from Manchester to Birkdale. Now the LYR operated over a much shorter route, the distance from Southport Chapel Street (LYR) to Liverpool being 18 miles compared with 31 miles on the CLC, while the distance to Manchester on the LYR was 37 miles compared with 50 on the CLC. Moreover, the LYR coastal route from Liverpool to Southport was electrified in 1904 providing an even faster service, while local tram services in the Southport area denied the SCLER any opportunity of capitalising on its service from the town centre to places such as Seaside and Birkdale.

In the post-Grouping era a number of schemes were put forward to improve the range of services offered, but nothing was done. The Southport directors, who still met despite their inability to authorise real changes without CLC approval, tried in vain to push through the complete amalgamation of the Southport Extension with the CLC in the hope that this would bring about better investment. But the LNER and LMS (with its rival interests at Chapel Street) would never consent to such a plan which could only have a negative effect on the CLC's accounts during a period when the Cheshire Lines itself was in financial difficulty. Similarly hopes that developments in the Liverpool area would result in a new lease of life for the Southport extension failed to materialise and in 1926 the press dubbed the SCLER the 'never never railway

Economies were made during the trade depression of the late 1920s and early 1930s by the use of a CLC Sentinel railcar but not even this could reverse falling traffic figures. A gradual decline in the number of passenger trains over the extension was a noticeable feature of the latter years of the CLC, and by 1945 the service had contracted to three stopping trains a day in each direction to Liverpool (with occasional lengthy delays at Gateacre) and two in each direction to Gateacre only — some of which connected with trains to Warrington, Manchester and Stockport. The express trains to Liverpool, Manchester and beyond were withdrawn long before, as was the LMS connection at Altcar, mainly through lack of use. Even so, the extension was valued by some commuters in Southport because of its direct connection with the networks of the CLC parent companies, and because of its through service to Manchester Central, which was more conveniently situated for business people who worked in the city than the rival LYR station at Victoria.

CHESHIRE LINES RAILWAY.

TOTAL ECLIPSE of the SUN

JUNE 29th, 1927.

On TUESDAY, JUNE 28th, for 2, 5 or 8 Days, and

WEDNESDAY, JUNE 29th, for 1 Day,

EXCURSION TRAINS will be run to

AINSDALE BEACH & SOUTHPORT

(LORD STREET STATION), as under:—

| | TIMES OF DEPARTURE | | RETURN FARES—THIRD CLASS. | | |
	Tuesday	Wednesday	AINSDALE BEACH 1 Day.	SOUTHPORT 1 Day.	2, 5 or 8 Days
Manchester (C.) ....dep.	6 10	8 15			
Trafford Park .... ,,	5 42	3 20			
Urmston .... ,,	5 48	3 25	4/3	4/3	5/9
Flixton .... ,,	5 54	3 30			
Irlam .... ,,	6 10	3 35			
Glazebrook .... ,,	6 15	3 39			
Ainsdale Beach ..arr.	7 32	4 35			
Southport (Lord St.) ,,	7 40	4 45			

†—Change at Warrington.
Children under 3 years of age, Free: 3 and under 12. Half-Fares.

xxxxxxxxxxxxxxxxxxxxxxxxxxxxxxxxxxxxxxxxxxxxxxxx

SOUTHPORT ATTRACTIONS.

ECLIPSE TIMES (Approx.) AT SOUTHPORT
BEGINS 5 30 a.m. - - ENDS 7 20 a.m.
TOTALITY at 6 24 a.m. for 23 SECONDS

SOUTHPORT IS THE ONLY SEASIDE HOLIDAY RESORT
ON THE CENTRAL LINE OF TOTALITY

Unlimited space for viewing the Eclipse from splendid vantage points is available on the Sandhills, Sea Embankments, etc., on the extensive foreshore free of charge.

ALL-NIGHT FESTIVITIES

The "Fairyland" illuminations in the Famous Lord Street Boulevards, in the South Marine Park, and at Pleasureland will remain on throughout the night of June 28th, and there will be a special Open-air Band Concert in the Municipal Gardens on June 29th, at 3 30 a.m.

Cafes, etc., will be Open for Early Morning Arrivals.

BAND PERFORMANCES DAILY by Famous Bands.

SOUTHPORT FOURTH ANNUAL GREAT FLOWER SHOW will take place in the Victoria Park on the 24th, 25th and 26th August, 1927. Over £4,000 in Trophies, Medals and Cash Prizes. Horse Leaping Contest, Sheep Dog Trials, Concerts by Military Bands.

SOUTHPORT FIFTH ANNUAL OPEN LAWN TENNIS TOURNAMENT will be held on the

Left: The last time that Britain experienced a total eclipse of the sun before 1999, Southport made much of its location on the line of totality; and of course the CLC got in on the act. To view the eclipse demanded an early start and there is a nice note about a train for businessmen who would like to get to Manchester in time for a normal day's work after witnessing it.

6

Other Centres

Stockport

Stockport was both the birthplace of the Cheshire Lines Committee and the point at which much of the traffic from the parent companies entered the system. The earliest sections of what became the CLC were incorporated by the MSLR and GNR to serve the town and these ultimately paved the way for later expansion and the introduction of the MR as the third partner.

The MSLR was attracted to Stockport by the prospect of extending its sphere of influence in the direction of Liverpool and by the proximity of its existing Manchester-Marple railway, which could easily be connected with the town via a short branch. Local interest in achieving rail access with the MSLR was considerable, especially as the Sheffield company promised to carry coal and merchandise at cheaper rates than the LNWR, whose near monopoly of local traffic was much resented. Consequently the MSLR supported a Bill promoted by landowners for the construction of a railway 2 miles 61 chains in length from Woodley Junction on the MSLR to the town centre. However, the MSLR was unable to raise the required capital and invited the GNR to enter into the venture. The Stockport & Woodley Junction Railway (SWJR) was incorporated on 15 May 1860, with the MSLR and GNR empowered to work the line and provide the capital, except for that subscribed by local interests.

Under Watkin's direction, the MSLR now saw an opportunity of furthering its ambitions and proposed that the SWJR should be extended to join the MSJAR and the Warrington & Stockport Railway (WSR — absorbed by LNWR in 1864), thereby providing a through route to north Cheshire and Liverpool, where the company had joint interests with the GNR. Once again, the MSLR was in no position to fund such a project and looked successfully to the Great Northern for financial support. The resulting Stockport, Timperley & Altrincham Junction Railway (STAJR) was authorised on 22 July 1861 to build a line 8 miles 47 chains from the SWJR to connect with the WSR at Broadheath Junction and the MSJAR at Timperley and Deansgate Junctions. A further junction was made at Northenden with the LNWR's Stockport to Altrincham line. The Act also authorised working arrangements with the SWJR and the Cheshire Midland Railway (MSLR & GNR Joint) and regulated running powers over the MSJAR. At the same time facilities were granted to the LNWR between Northenden and Broadheath Junctions. The working arrangements between the GNR and MSLR were formally authorised under the Great Northern (Cheshire Lines) Act of 13 July 1863, which covered other jointly owned lines in Lancashire and Cheshire and which became the basis of the CLC.

Right: In wartime LNER livery, 'J10' 0-6-0 No 5154 approaches Godley from Woodley on the east spur of the CLC line from Stockport Tiviot Dale to the GC main line. This was the CLC's crucial link with the LNER system. *P. Ward*

Left: Woodley station on 16 January 1950, with a passenger train running in. *Oliver Carter*

Below: Stockport Tiviot Dale station with ARP emergency water signs still painted on the gate post, despite it being well into the 1950s. The handsome station building included an almost ecclesiastical arcade along its frontage. *Stockport Museums & Art Gallery Service*

Left: Tiviot Dale from the up platform on 26 August 1947. Apart from the famous arched footbridge, points of interest include the decorative lamp posts and the double ground signals. The spare switches and crossings between the tracks were placed there as emergency spares in case of bomb damage; their rail ends are painted white to help staff see them in the black-out. *William J. Skillern/ Author's Collection*

Above: The signalbox and a fine bracket signal at the east end of Tiviot Dale, looking towards Woodley on 14 April 1961. Signs of change are in the background, with rubble-filled gaps where mills used to stand.
R. E. Gee

Construction of the SWJR was slow, due to engineering difficulties, tunnelling work and the provision of a masonry viaduct near Woodley. The railway was finally opened to passengers in January 1863 and a temporary station provided at Stockport Portwood. There were no intermediate stations and no accommodation for goods. Initially receipts were poor and for the half year ending December 1864 the SWJR made a loss of £1,400.

Meanwhile, work was progressing on the STAJR and a grand opening was set for the summer of 1865 to coincide with the official launch of the newly titled Cheshire Lines Committee (5 June 1865). However, the line failed to pass inspection, as a number of bridges needed to be strengthened and various improvements made to the permanent way. Instead, a local opening was made on 1 December 1865 from Portwood to Deansgate Junction, the only station then ready for use being Stockport Teviot Dale (spelling later altered to Tiviot), which became the CLC's principal station in the town. At the same time, goods facilities were introduced at Portwood station. Additional stations followed in February 1866 at Baguley, Northenden (for Wythenshawe) and Cheadle.

February 1866 also saw the opening of the section between Broadheath and Skelton (East) Junctions, and the construction of a short branch from Apethorne Junction on the SMJC Romiley–Hyde line near Woodley, to Godley Junction on the MSLR main line to Sheffield. The branch was built by the MSLR but transferred to the CLC in August 1866, owing to the reasonable refusal of the GNR to pay half the costs of erecting a new station at Godley (as demanded by Watkin) unless the line became jointly owned. The branch was reached from Stockport via a short break of 27 chains between Woodley and Apethorne Junctions, where the CLC traversed the SMJC. Two branches of 20 and 10 chains each were laid at Stockport during the same year to serve Wellington Road and St George's Road goods stations.

Further connections were made with the SMJC in 1875 at Brinnington and Bredbury Junctions, thereby giving the Midland Railway access to Manchester via Tiviot Dale, and thus increasing the range of services offered from the station. However, the number of connections in the Stockport area could also have adverse effects on the CLC. In April 1877, the Committee consulted its solicitors to clarify the legality of LNWR trains stopping at Northenden station on their way between Northenden and Broadheath Junctions. To the CLC's frustration, it was found that the terms of the 1861 Act enabled the North Western to pick up and put down passengers for through trains to destinations such as Liverpool but it had no right to use the station for local traffic.

Clearly, this was a very difficult situation to regulate and many passengers continued to use the LNWR for local services to and from Northenden.

Tensions between rival companies could also spill over into the conduct of staff. In August 1877 Mr W. Etchells, the CLC Signalman at Woodley West box, was dismissed for fighting with an SMJC shunter following a disagreement over a signalling decision! Surprisingly, such loutish behaviour was not uncommon, as a perusal of the CLC minute books for the period reveals an almost monthly list of dismissals for drunkenness, insubordination and theft.

Services between Tiviot Dale and Manchester were greatly improved in 1879 following the opening of the MSLR's Skelton Loop (otherwise known as the Timperley Curve), which joined the MSJAR south of Timperley station and the CLC at Skelton North Junction. This route was itself superseded in 1881 by the opening of Heaton Mersey East Junction, just north of Tiviot Dale station, which thus provided direct access to Central via the South District Railway. Nevertheless, considering the proximity of Stockport to Manchester, the CLC route was long and slow and from the start suffered from competition with the 'penny tramcar'. The original Skelton Loop was removed by the GCR in 1903.

A second junction with the MR was made at Cheadle in 1902, following the opening of the Midland's new approach to Manchester Central via Chinley and Cheadle Heath. Tiviot Dale undoubtedly suffered as a result, as Midland trains could now bypass the town on their way to and from Manchester and Liverpool. Even so, by the early years of the 20th century the CLC was able to offer a range of services from Tiviot Dale similar in scope to those available from Manchester, as many of the parent companies' through trains continued to use the station. Local services were just as important, especially with the growth of commuter traffic. Baguley was noted as a pretty residential area famous for its market gardens, while Northenden was described by *Railway & Travel Monthly* in 1913 as, 'a sort of Hampstead Heath for Manchester, particularly on Bank Holidays, the river being available for boating for several miles'.

From the perspective of the CLC, goods traffic was equally, if not more, important than passenger traffic, and the Committee had accounts with many of the local industries, such as the cotton mills and hat manufacturers for which the town was once famous. The CLC's connections in the Manchester area, and especially the junctions at Godley, Northenden and Cheadle, meant that Stockport was an important centre for through goods trains. The original SWJR station at Portwood was converted to solely goods and minerals in September 1875. Additional goods lines were brought into use on 29 November 1880 between Portwood and Brinnington Junctions and on 15 March 1881 between Heaton Mersey West Junction and St George's Road. Large marshalling sidings were also laid at Heaton Mersey and completed early in 1882. New interchange sidings were provided at Cheadle Junction when the MR line from Cheadle Heath opened in 1902.

Meanwhile, facilities at Wellington Road and St George's Road had developed considerably, and by the early 1900s there were signs that both sites had reached their capacity. However, the parent companies were reluctant to authorise new

Right: The competition. The LNWR station at Cheadle was much nearer the town centre than the CLC station but somehow never bothered to make the best of this opportunity. Although some desultory attempts were made to poach traffic, the station generally had a poor service and was not well patronised: it was closed in 1917.
Author's Collection

Centre right: Altrincham station was a junction, where the CLC met the Manchester South Junction & Altrincham from Oxford Road. The MSJAR platforms are on the left, while a CLC train waits behind GC No 170 on the right. Note the bracket signal extending out through the station canopy.
David Bownes Collection

Below: At Northwich the CLC shared an island platform with the LNWR. It is just visible to the right, with a paltry canopy compared to the main (CLC) platform opposite; when the CLC wanted to refurbish the station the LNWR refused to pay its share of the cost, so the island platform was left as it was. *Author's Collection*

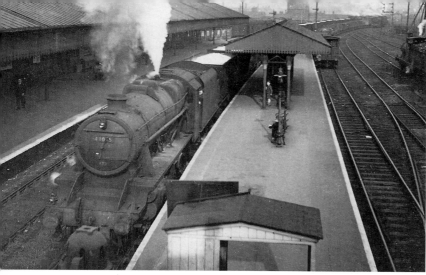

Left: A heavy limestone train rumbles through Northwich in April 1954, '8F' No 48045 working hard and blowing off vigorously. *P. Ward*

Below left: At the rear of the train another '8F' banks the load up the climb towards Hartford. *P. Ward*

expenditure and often rejected plans submitted by the CLC. New warehouse accommodation was eventually provided at Stockport in 1908 and improvements were made over the years at Wellington Road and St George's Road goods stations.

During World War 1, additional sidings were put in at Heaton Mersey, because of the increased traffic destined for Brunner Mond & Co (chemical manufacturers) and John Summers & Sons Ltd (steel manufacturers), which passed through Stockport on its way to Northwich and Chester. Indeed, the section between Northenden and Skelton Junctions became one of the busiest stretches of double track in the country and effectively served as the goods avoiding line for Manchester.

After the depression of the 1920s, services in the Stockport area again began to blossom and in 1936 plans were promoted by the Wythenshawe Committee of Manchester Corporation for the electrification of the CLC between Timperley Junction and Northenden and the LMS Wilmslow line, thereby extending the electric service to Manchester offered by the MSJAR. The LMS and LNER were never in favour and finally scuppered the scheme by claiming that they could not compete with bus companies offering services from these districts to the city centre.

Considering the importance of Stockport for goods traffic, Tiviot Dale and the Wellington Road/St George's Road goods depots were fortunate to avoid damage during the 1939-45 war. Among the more unusual traffic carried at

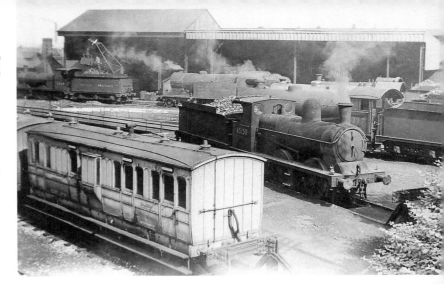

Right: Northwich MPD on 10 July 1949, with a fine array of ex-GC motive power on shed. In the foreground old carriages are seeing out their last days as mobile staff accommodation.
N. R. Knight/P. Ward Collection

Below right: The motive power allocation, though not the buildings, has changed by 1954, when a rather unkempt '8F' No 48254 is being coaled.
P Ward

that time were prisoner of war specials, which ran through the middle lines of Stockport Tiviot Dale en route from Hull to Liverpool and Canada.

Northwich

As with Stockport, the opening of the CLC line to Northwich predated the formation of the Committee. The MSLR was keen to gain access to the growing chemical and salt mining industries of the Northwich area but was unable to fund the project by itself. Instead, it proposed to extend the MSJAR (which it owned jointly with the LNWR) from its terminus at Altrincham to Northwich (a distance of 12 miles 65 chains) and supported a local Bill to that effect. The Cheshire Midland Railway (CMR), as it was known, received Parliamentary approval on 14 June 1860, with a

capital of £100,000 divided into 5,000 shares of £20 each. By this Act the MSLR and LNWR were empowered to enter into working agreements and to subscribe capital to the undertaking. However, the LNWR failed to exercise the powers conferred on it and the MSLR was authorised to make a further contribution to the CMR capital in 1861. To fund this the MSLR entered into a working agreement with the GNR, which placed the CMR on the same footing as other railways jointly owned by the two companies in Liverpool and Stockport.

The first section of the CMR opened from Altrincham (MSJAR) to Knutsford for passengers on 12 May 1862, with intermediate stations at Bowden Peel Causeway (renamed Hale in 1902), Ashley (for Rostherne) and Mobberley. The second

Above: Mineral traffic in connection with the chemical industry was a vital part of the CLC's lifeblood trade. This view shows a part of the extensive ICI sidings complex at Northwich. *P. Ward*

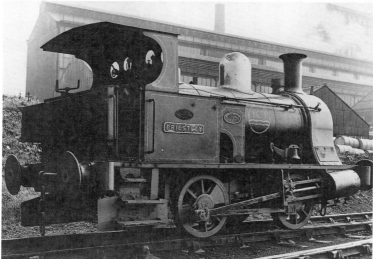

Left: ICI possessed an interesting fleet of industrial shunters for use around the works and in the sidings. *Priestley* was a Kerr Stuart 0-4-0WT of 1912, seen here at Winnington in October 1954. *IC Mond Division*

phase from Knutsford to Northwich followed on 1 January 1863, with stations at Plumbley (spelling altered to Plumley in 1945) and Lostock Gralam. Goods traffic commenced on 1 May 1863, and from December 1867 several short branches were opened in the vicinity of Northwich to serve the town's numerous salt works. An initial passenger service of five trains in each direction was run on weekdays, with four on Sundays. Later services traversed the MSJAR to reach Manchester (Oxford Road) and continued to use this route to Manchester following the opening of Central station in 1880. Consequently, the CLC

paid a user charge for Altrincham station, which in 1883 stood at £250 per annum, and maintained a close relationship with the MSJAR throughout its existence.

The original station and goods accommodation at Northwich were of temporary wooden construction, as it was realised that a much larger station would be needed once the West Cheshire extension was opened (authorised in July 1861). The WCR Act also sanctioned important junctions with the LNWR at Northwich (for Sandbach) and Hartford (with the Crewe-Liverpool main line). As the first of these junctions was due to open

Above: Warrington Central's rather grand façade has been somewhat overlooked over the years, as it is not immediately apparent to the traveller arriving either by rail or road. The main public entrance was at road level to the right of this view and a new entrance hall has bypassed the older buildings most effectively.
Peter Norton/Author's Collection

before the rest of the WCR, work began on a second station during 1867, and this was brought into use at the end of May 1868. The new station was positioned to the south of the existing one, which was eventually demolished and the site used for Northwich goods depot. The LNWR branch from Sandbach opened for goods in November 1867 and for passengers during the following July. CLC services from the new station commenced in September 1869 for goods, and June 1870 for passengers, following the completion of the WCR to Helsby & Alvanley.

The most important engineering feature of the WCR was the viaduct between Northwich and Hartford, which carried the railway over the Dane and Weaver rivers, the Weaver Canal and low-lying land, on 48 stone arches and two wrought-iron girder bridges, giving a total length of over half a mile.

On 1 June 1870 a short branch was opened for goods only from Hartford to Winnington, to serve the chemical works of Brunner Mond & Co. Although a mere 1 mile 63 chains in length, the branch had a gradient of 1 in 53 — the stiffest on the system. Rail access was also established with Brunner Mond's factory at Lostock Gralam and with other salt works in the Northwich area. Industry as a whole expanded rapidly during this period, and improvements were made at Northwich by the construction of additional

sidings and station amenities in 1876, a new engine shed in 1877, a new warehouse and goods offices in 1880 and the introduction of the block system from Mouldsworth in July 1886. This was undoubtedly a boom time for Northwich, built on the success of the chemical and salt industries. Hence, when describing the Cheshire section of the CLC in 1899, the *Railway Magazine* broke from its prosaic description of the countryside around Knutsford and Plumbley to portray the scene greeting the passenger at Lostock Gralam:

'...[here] the face of nature has been wholly spoiled by hideous erections for the manufacture of chemicals, but these are not unsightly objects to the railway shareholder, who sees increased traffic and revenue in every addition to the already large community of works which have gradually extended until they really form part of Northwich, the next town, which, as everyone knows, is remarkable for its extensive salt mines and salt springs which abound in the neighbourhood.'

In 1908 a connection was made at Plumbley West with the Holford Hall works of the Ammonia Soda Company (later absorbed by Brunner Mond) following the discovery of unprecedented reserves of brine at the site. Extra sidings were authorised for Northwich in connection with the chemical industry during 1912, as it was found that engines spent up to 24 hours a day performing shunting duties in order to keep the main line clear — a state of affairs which inevitably resulted in delays to all types of traffic.

In the meantime, passenger services from Northwich had dramatically increased both in scope and frequency. Under an agreement made in 1868 the LNWR was granted facilities at

Northwich station and the use of the Committee's line between Northwich and Hartford Junction. From March 1870 the LNWR (and later LMS) exercised these running powers with local passenger services from Northwich to Liverpool Lime Street and Earlestown, and with summer excursions from Sandbach to Blackpool. In addition, the LNWR operated a frequent passenger service to Northwich from Sandbach and Crewe via Sandbach Junction, which was also the route by which the North Staffordshire was reached. Thus by 1894 the LNWR ran an average of 26 passenger trains a day to and from Northwich (compared to 30 CLC services), including a through service from Manchester (Oxford Road) to London Euston via Altrincham, Northwich, Sandbach and Crewe, which was later discontinued.

Inevitably the LNWR's use of Northwich station led to occasional tension between the two companies, especially as the North Western repeatedly refused to improve facilities on the down platform, which it shared with the CLC. Matters came to a head in 1896 when, following numerous complaints from passengers, the CLC spent a considerable sum on widening, lengthening and covering the up platform (to Manchester) and providing additional waiting room and office accommodation, only to be thwarted in its attempt to do the same for the

Chester platform by the parsimonious attitude of the LNWR. Despite an angry exchange of letters, nothing could be done, due to the joint use of the platform and, rather unfairly, the CLC continued to receive complaints from disgruntled customers.

By 1910, Northwich was an extremely busy part of the system. As well as the large number of CLC goods and passenger trains which used the station, many of which started from Northwich in the direction of either Chester or Manchester, there was a constant stream of mineral and goods trains from the MR and GCR, as well as passengers, goods and cattle from the LNWR and a daily mineral train from the NSR (ex Cliff Vale).

During World War 1 additional siding accommodation was provided at Northwich and Plumbley to cater for increased traffic arising out of the war effort, to and from the works of Brunner Mond at Lostock and Winnington. Temporary 'stations' were built at Plumbley West and Lostock sidings to service munitions factories established at these locations for the duration of the war. An initial service of workmen's trains was put on from Manchester Central and Altrincham to Lostock (Temporary Platform). In November 1917 the service was expanded to enable workmen's trains to run through to Plumbley West from Winsford & Over, calling at Whitegate, Cuddington, Hartford & Greenbank and

Left: Wigan was the limit of Great Central influence in the Northwest, the end of a line which left the CLC at Glazebrook. Wigan Central was served by regular services from Manchester Central, operated as an integral part of the CLC timetable. The station is seen on 18 April 1960, when it had entered a state of crumbling decline. The long canopy and touches of grand architectural flourishes on the buildings behind speak of earlier high hopes and the style with which Watkin liked to see his railways invade other territory. *T. Lewis*

Right: CLC land and the station at Helsby, showing the site of Helsby & Alvanley station, also part of the connecting spur with the LNWR, top left.
CLC Official Map/ Author's Collection

CHESHIRE LINES.
URGENT 186
From HELSBY, C.L.C.
To YORK, N.E.
Via GODLEY, SWINTON & KNOTTINGLEY
TOTAL NUMBER OF SHEETS
IN or ON Wagon
Owner and No. of Wagon
Consignee

Northwich. The frequency of this service was reduced during 1918 and by 1 January 1919 there was only one weekday train each way from Manchester to Plumbley West and Lostock, with none on Sundays. The service was discontinued in April 1919 and the temporary stations closed.

In the postwar period, freight trains were increased between Warrington, Northwich and Middlewich (LMS), and a specialised circuit introduced for the conveyance of limestone from the Peak District in Derbyshire to the Alkali Division works of ICI (which had taken over Brunner Mond) at Lostock and Winnington. To handle this traffic, a fleet of limestone hoppers, each capable of carrying 43½ tons, was built for ICI by Charles Roberts from 1935.

A new passenger service from Northwich to Birkenhead was also introduced during the 1930s (see below). However, following the outbreak of war in 1939, many services were discontinued (including trains to Liverpool Lime Street via Hartford Junction), and the line to Sandbach was used only for the passage of troops and freight. A new connection was put in at Plumbley West with the factory of the British Ethyl Corporation in 1940/1, and increased demands were placed on the Northwich chemical industry for the production of chemicals used in the manufacture of munitions. By 1945 the total amount of freight in and out of the ICI works had soared to over two million tons, most of which was carried by the CLC.

Northwich remained a major centre for the chemical industry after the war. On the eve of nationalisation in 1947, the CLC was running up to nine limestone trains a day, each loaded to 16 wagons, between Tunstead and Winnington. This, combined with the volume of goods and salt traffic dealt with, ensured that Northwich was the busiest station on the CLC's Cheshire section.

Warrington

Warrington Central opened for goods and passenger traffic during the summer of 1873, as part of the Liverpool to Manchester main line. New stations were also opened in the direction of Liverpool at Hough Green (for Ditton), Farnworth (for Widnes) and Sankey (for Penketh), and in the direction of Manchester at Padgate. The original route, authorised in 1865, sited Warrington station on what became known as the 'Straight Line' (or Warrington avoiding line to give it its proper title) between Sankey and Padgate junctions. However, public agitation resulted in powers being obtained in 1866 for the construction of a loop between these two junctions, which enabled the station to be located closer to the town centre. Although the loop opened in 1873, the Straight Line was not brought into use until 1883.

From the start a wide variety of passenger services was available from Warrington to all parts of the CLC, while many of the parent companies' through trains called at the town on their way to and from Liverpool. Commuters and business people were especially well served, as both the CLC's Liverpool-Manchester express and the MR's London-Liverpool Pullman Service (introduced in 1875) stopped at Warrington Central. Local services flourished and following the opening of the SCLER in 1884, regular trains were provided to Southport via Halewood and Aintree. Similarly, frequent trains were run to Wigan and St Helens via the junction at Glazebrook with the Wigan Junction Railway (later absorbed by the GCR), and to Widnes via a junction with the SMJC between Farnworth and Sankey.

At Warrington, extensive goods facilities and a number of branches were constructed to serve local industries. A connection with Dallam & Bewsey Forges was opened in June 1873, followed in 1874 by a short branch at Whitecross to serve the wire factory, and later an iron foundry of the same name. Coaling sidings were installed at

Battersby Lane, which were enlarged in 1905 and again in 1912 following the opening of the Partington Steel and Iron Co. Meanwhile, a small locomotive shed was built near to the Whitecross branch, and a substantial goods warehouse erected in the main CLC goods yard adjacent to the station.

The Battersby Lane spur also served the Cheshire Lines' workshops and stores, which incorporated the rolling stock repair, printing and signal works. The first workshops were built in about 1881, and gradually expanded over the years at a site on the corner of Battersby Lane and Marsh House Lane. The Cheshire Lines' stores at Battersby Lane were under the jurisdiction of the storekeeper, a senior position in the company's hierarchy, which was held from 1888 to the early years of the 20th century by Mr S. Saxon Barton. Together with the signalling works and general repair/fabrication shops, they were taken over by the LMS towards the end of the 1930s.

During World War 2, Warrington Goods Yard became the scene of frenetic activity. The 'straight line' was used for a while as additional sidings for goods destined for Liverpool, and all other traffic diverted via the loop. At Risley, on the main line between Warrington and Manchester, a new station with siding accommodation was opened on 2 April 1940 to serve the Ordnance Factory, and a new siding put in at Burtonwood to connect with the RAF Maintenance Unit (later transferred to the American Air Force).

Helsby

In July 1861 the MSLR and GNR obtained powers under the West Cheshire Railway Act to extend the Cheshire Midland Railway from Northwich to Helsby & Alvanley, a distance of 14 miles 30 chains, with intermediate stations at Hartford & Greenbank, Cuddington, Delamere, Mouldsworth and Manley. The new railway, which became part of the CLC in 1865, opened for goods on 1 September 1869 and began carrying passengers the following June.

The primary objective of the new line was to form a junction at Helsby with the Birkenhead Joint Railway (GWR & LNWR), but construction work beyond Helsby & Alvanley station took longer than expected, due to the boggy nature of the ground there. A connection, known as the West Cheshire Junction, was eventually opened on 14 June 1871, giving the CLC access to Birkenhead, Ellesmere Port and other parts of the BJR's network.

Passenger services from Helsby initially consisted of through trains to Manchester Oxford Road, but following the opening of the CLC's

Right: By running powers and joint agreements, the CLC managed to get a pincer-hold on the Mersey port area, with bases in both Liverpool and Birkenhead. This is Birkenhead passenger station shortly after World War 1; even a casual glance at the picture betrays that it was a facility provided on the cheap, seriously disgraced by the style and scale of Liverpool Central across the river.
J. A. Peden/GCRS Collection

extension to Chester in 1875, the section from Mouldsworth Junction to the Birkenhead Joint was effectively transformed into a goods branch, and passenger facilities withdrawn from Helsby & Alvanley and Manley stations.

At first, the Cheshire Lines hoped to obtain running powers through to Birkenhead but as these were not forthcoming, all trains had to change engines at Helsby (West Cheshire Junction). To facilitate this, a two-road engine shed was authorised for Helsby in May 1891 and brought into operation during 1893, with locomotives supplied from the main shed at Northwich. During the General Strike of 1926, Helsby Shed achieved the unique distinction of being the only CLC depot to remain fully active, despite severe coal shortages. However, together with Winsford, the shed was closed in 1929 as an economy measure, and the rosters taken over by Northwich.

Apart from being an important junction for CLC traffic, Helsby was used by the LNWR (later LMS) and GWR to transfer goods to parts of Cheshire and elsewhere. The GWR in particular exchanged a large proportion of its heavy traffic destined for Liverpool at the West Cheshire Junction, as it had no direct access of its own to the docks. The CLC also had an important connection at Helsby with the factories of the British Insulated Cable Co, which were connected with the CLC sidings by a narrow gauge tramway operated by a petrol tractor. Other local traffic on the Helsby Branch came from Manley Quarry, which was served by a short branch.

Helsby & Alvanley station was reopened for passengers in May 1934 and used intermittently during the summer months for services between Birkenhead and Northwich (some of which went on to Knutsford), and on a daily basis for workmen's trains between Hooton and Helsby — presumably to serve the factories of the British Insulated Cable Co. In 1937 the LMS offered passenger services from Northwich to Birkenhead (Woodside), calling at Hartford, Cuddington, Delamere, Mouldsworth, Helsby, Ince, Ellesmere Port, Little Sutton, Hooton, Bromborough, Spital, Port Sunlight, Bebington and Rock Ferry. These trains were formed of GWR stock hauled by LMS engines, and ran up to the outbreak of war. Workmen's services survived until 22 May 1944.

During World War 2, running line facilities were greatly augmented between Mouldsworth and Helsby, to cater for the heavy oil traffic from Ellesmere Port and shipping traffic for Birkenhead Docks, which constituted the main types of goods carried on the line during its final years under CLC control.

Birkenhead

The Cheshire Lines' dockside developments at Birkenhead were never physically connected with the rest of the Committee's system. Instead, they were reached via a junction with the BJR at Helsby (see previous section), whose parent companies received running powers over the CLC in return. In this way the CLC was able to gain a share of the valuable shipping traffic using the docks, and thus establish a presence on the south bank of the Mersey.

The CLC's earliest development in Birkenhead was at Shore Road, which was situated on the north side of the main docks, where the Committee leased land from the Mersey Docks & Harbour Board (MDHB). A depot was opened there for goods only in July 1871 and joined the Birkenhead Joint at Brook Street Junction. Further connections with the dock lines of the MDHB were made in September 1875. At first all

Above: An early post-Grouping view of Birkenhead Shore Road Goods station and the fan of lines leading through the roads to major sources of traffic. The state of the cobbled road surface is something to ponder. *National Railway Museum*

traffic was hauled by horses but by 1883 the amount of goods handled at the depot had risen so dramatically (from 24,000 tons in 1872 to 138,000 tons) that it was decided to employ the services of a shunting engine. Further increases in traffic led to the introduction of an extra locomotive and the construction of an engine shed in 1888, although heavy shunting horses continued to be used well into the post-Grouping era.

Facilities at the goods station were significantly enhanced between 1889-92, with the construction of new offices, an impressive warehouse, and improvements to the track layout and engine shed. At this time, one of the most important sources of revenue at Shore Road was from the export of cattle to Canada, which were loaded at Birkenhead owing to restrictions placed on the Lancashire side of the Mersey by the Privy Council. As the CLC had no lairage of its own, cattle pens were leased from the MDHB at Alfred Docks for this purpose.

Aware of the growing potential of Birkenhead Docks and eager to safeguard against the possible termination of its lease at Shore Road, the Cheshire Lines purchased land at Seacombe in 1891 to construct its own dock frontage. As ever, Watkin was keen to push the scheme further and tried to persuade his partners in the CLC to use the newly acquired land to link Birkenhead with the south end of Liverpool via the underground Mersey Railway. Apart from easing the shipment of goods from Birkenhead to Lancashire (which were currently routed through Helsby and Cornbrook), the MSLR also sought to provide a physical connection with the North Wales & Liverpool Railway, in which it had an interest. However, the Midland and Great Northern directors would not agree to the scheme and it

was eventually dropped. The CLC depot, known as East & West Float, was brought into use during November 1892, with access to it achieved over the dock lines to the Wirral Railway and Birkenhead Joint. At the turn of the century the GCR tried once more to connect the site with other parts of its system, and to introduce better goods facilities with the intention of superseding those at Shore Road. The proposals were again blocked by the Midland and Great Northern companies, causing a great deal of ill feeling between the partners.

Traffic at both sites continued to grow steadily during the late 19th and early 20th centuries and, despite the efforts of the Great Central, Shore Road remained the CLC's principal goods station in Birkenhead and offered direct rail access (via the MDHB lines) to several of the adjoining docks and lairages. In this way, the CLC was able to ship goods of all types to destinations such as India, China, Japan, Burma and South Africa. Meanwhile, East & West Float developed a significant traffic in timber and oil cake, and was substantially enlarged during World War 1 to deal with the heavy tonnage of war material passing through the port. Similarly, both depots experienced a dramatic increase in traffic following the outbreak of war in 1939, which was further stimulated by the opening of an additional junction with the BJR at Mickle Trafford to cope with the transfer of goods to and from Birkenhead Docks.

7

The Winsford Branch

In terms of passenger traffic the West Cheshire main line between Northwich and Helsby was the least profitable stretch of the company's network and the Winsford Branch in particular was notorious for its failure to show a profit. When questioned about the branch in 1891, the chief engineer of the CLC claimed that the line had always been regarded by the company as a mineral railway, serving what the then manager David Meldrum referred to as the 'non-competitive' route to Chester. However, had the original aims of Watkin, the railway's promoter, come to fruition, the story might have been very different, as the Winsford Branch would have acted as the springboard for a bold policy of expansion into southeast Cheshire and beyond.

The CLC was initially attracted to Winsford by the prospect of tapping into the lucrative salt trade. At the time practically all the salt manufactured in the region, together with the coal used in its production, was carried by the Weaver Navigation. This monopoly was jealously guarded by the Weaver Trustees, who vigorously opposed the CLC's attempt to serve the mines direct. However, Watkin found a powerful ally in the influential salt proprietor Herman Eugene Falk, who was prepared to support the West Cheshire

Railway Bill in return for an assurance that the Winsford Branch would terminate at a junction with his Meadowbank Works.

Falk's support proved crucial in securing the passage of the Bill through Parliament, although the CLC later disregarded its promise to him and extended the branch to serve rival salt manufacturers. Even so, there remained a number of workings on the opposite bank of the Weaver which the company was unable to reach. Anxious to prevent this lucrative traffic remaining in the hands of the LNWR (whose main line ran close by), the CLC proposed in 1875 to build a bridge over the river for the use of salt trains only. The proposal was flatly rejected by the parent companies.

Authorised under the West Cheshire Act (1862), the Winsford Branch was built by the firm of Benton & Woodiwiss between 1866 and 1868 for the sum of £23,646 13s 6d, exclusive of stations and buildings. A single line throughout, the railway ran from a junction with the main line near Cuddington to a point close to Meadowbank Works — a distance of 5¼miles. Additional land was subsequently purchased from Lord Delamere to extend the railway into the centre of Winsford and so give greater access both to the travelling

Right: An undated view of Whitegate station, taken from the signalbox. The tall semaphore signals and goods loop on the right of the passenger line were put in as part of the Board of Trade's recommendations in 1891/2.
David Bownes Collection

public and to the numerous salt workings clustered about the banks of the River Weaver.

The contract for the Winsford extension again went to Messrs Benton & Woodiwiss, whose tender for £14,462 18s 1d was significantly lower than that of its rivals. But the expenditure was far from over. A number of sidings were put in to serve the salt workings at an average cost of £500 each. £370 was spent on repairing the approach road to Winsford & Over station and more than £1,000 was required to supply the new engine shed and station buildings with water. Further expenditure was also necessitated by subsidence caused by brine pumping, a problem which was to bedevil the branch throughout its existence. The total cost of the line, including a station at Whitegate, several crossing cottages and the original purchase of the land, was put at £150,000 or approximately £25,000 for each of the 6½ miles constituting its final length.

The completed railway was opened to goods traffic on 1 June 1870 and to passengers a month later. It was an immediate failure as far as passenger services were concerned. They were withdrawn from 1 January 1874 but restarted for a trial period in May 1886. Following an accident, the line was again closed to passengers in 1888 and would have remained so, had not the CLC been forced by an order of the Court of the Railway & Canal Commission to reintroduce facilities in 1892.

What had gone wrong? On the face of it the Winsford Branch never looked like being a paying proposition as far as passenger traffic was concerned. Its intermediate station at Whitegate served a small rural community, while the terminus at Winsford had to compete with the LNWR main line to Liverpool and Manchester (via Warrington) for patronage from a more or less static population of 10,000 inhabitants. Indeed, apart from local traffic and business generated by the salt industry, the CLC was reduced to extolling the restorative virtues of Winsford brine baths as practically the sole reason for visiting the town.

In fact Watkin had never intended that the railway would terminate at Winsford. This is evident from the 'temporary' appearance of the facilities there. For although the small village of Whitegate was provided with a brick-built station, the townspeople of Winsford had to make do with a wooden structure removed from Northwich station during its refurbishment in 1868. Even the original warehouse and engine shed at Winsford were constructed from old timbers recovered from the redevelopment at Northwich. Under Watkin's scheme, Winsford station would eventually have been upgraded and the railway extended to join the North Staffordshire line near Sandbach but he was unable to persuade his partners in the CLC to adopt the plan. Undaunted, he went ahead alone and secured enough local support for the Sandbach & Winsford Junction Railway to be incorporated on 27 June 1872. The Midland and Great Northern directors would still have nothing to do with the project and within three years it was abandoned.

A second attempt to extend the branch was

Left: The working of the Sentinel steam railcar brought the branch additional interest and attention in its last years. The railcar spent 18 months (July 1929-December 1930) on the line; this damaged but historically important picture shows it at Whitegate. By this time much of the original station furniture had gone, although a standard CLC lantern and the replacement concrete running-in board are prominent.
Cheshire County Council

Above right: Winsford & Over station in 1910. A passenger train headed by GCR 2-4-0 No 169 waits to depart for Cuddington. Addition of the name of a nearby community to a station's title was fairly common practice with CLC rural stations.
Winsford Local History Society

Centre right: Cuddington was the junction from the branch on the main Chester line. The Sentinel railcar is seen standing there in 1930. *Locomotive & General Railway Publications*

Below right: Some 20 years after the branch had closed to passenger traffic, the running-in boards still invited passengers to change for its services — though this could have been left up as a reference to the replacement bus service! Fairburn '4MT' 2-6-4T No 42676 runs into the station with an early evening Manchester-Chester train on 15 June 1952.
J. D. Darby

Left: An unidentified 'J10' heads a long freight train, formed mainly of sheeted open wagons, past Cuddington station's holding loops in 1948. *L&GRP*

Right: The Salt Union ran its own wagon building and repair shops at Winsford; this rare view shows maintenance in hand in the early 1920s. Private-owner wagons might have saved the railway companies money but they were generally as basic as possible and the refusal of their owners to modernise kept railway freight operations trapped in a mid-19th century timewarp until the 1960s. *Northwich Salt Museum*

made in 1883, when it was proposed to connect the CLC with the Cambrian Railways at Whitchurch and the Great Western at Nantwich, via a junction with Winsford. Although not sponsored by the CLC, the Whitchurch, Nantwich & Cheshire Lines Junction Railway Bill received the company's full support and was put before Parliament in 1884. This time it was the Bill itself which proved unsuccessful and the CLC had to wait another six years before the MSLR's extension to Chester Northgate gave it a link with the Cambrian.

Though the failure of these schemes was regarded as a disappointment by the empire-building MSLR, the real losers were the people of Winsford. Without a more popular destination, the Winsford Branch was never going to be more than a side-show for the CLC and the quality of the resulting passenger service reflected this. Indeed the CLC made little secret of its desire to withdraw passenger facilities altogether and, in the early years at least, paid scant regard to either the comfort or safety of its passengers.

When the line opened in 1870, the CLC put on a service of three mixed trains in each direction between Winsford and Cuddington, where passengers were obliged to change before continuing their journey. Receipts had been so poor that the service was withdrawn at the end of 1873. Under pressure from the Winsford Local Board and mindful that the newly opened extension to Chester (1875) might result in increased revenue, the CLC reintroduced the same service for a trial period in 1886. The 6½-mile journey was scheduled to take 20 minutes but delays were commonplace, as the antiquated coaches were continually shunted in and out of the sidings along the way to pick up and put down goods wagons. The coaches themselves were

described by passengers in 1891 as being 'very bad', 'very poor' and 'very dirty' and the incessant delays caused many to leave the coaches at the sidings and complete their journeys on foot. One farmer who used the passenger train to transport milk, complained that his produce was often ruined before it reached market on account of the constant jolting of the trains which, he added, were so slow that he could easily walk from his farm at Whitegate to Cuddington in less time.

Quite apart from the inconvenience suffered by passengers, the branch was worked in a manner which made the handling of such traffic positively dangerous. The staff and ticket system was in operation but the many sidings at Winsford were not interlocked and had been constructed without the approval of the Board of Trade, on land which had been purchased and developed without Parliamentary sanction. It was, to use the well-worn phrase, 'an accident waiting to happen'. On 25 August 1888 a typical Winsford train, consisting of an engine and tender, two passenger coaches, seven empty coal wagons and a break [sic] van, collided with 18 empty wagons on an unguarded siding. Fortunately there were no serious injuries.

An investigation into the accident revealed that responsibility for placing the junction points right for the main line had been placed in the hands of the number taker (a 17-year-old lad), rather than either the guard or shunter, whose job it was. This kind of sloppy working practice reflected the discipline problems experienced at Winsford, which had seen several shunters dismissed for offences ranging from poor timekeeping to drunkenness and vandalism. In his report for the Board of Trade, Colonel F. H. Rich was critical of both the CLC for putting profits before safety and the station staff who had contributed to the

Above: The branch had lost its passenger service and Winsford station was becoming rather dilapidated by the time the RCTS paid a visit by special train, in the form of a push-pull set. *R. M. Casserley Collection*

accident by 'carelessness in carrying out their respective duties'. He recommended that the sidings in connection with the branch should 'be rearranged, resignalled and [that] the points should be interlocked'. The CLC refused to implement the recommendations, on the grounds that the passenger traffic estimated at less than 42 journeys a day did not warrant the expense, and the service was withdrawn.

Yet despite the appalling facilities offered by the CLC, the service was valued in a locality where the only alternative means of travelling to towns like Northwich or Chester involved the even slower horse-drawn omnibus or the much more circuitous route offered by the LNWR, whose station at Winsford was inconveniently situated outside the town centre. In response to these considerations the Winsford Local Board brought an action against the CLC before the Court of the Railway & Canal Commission in

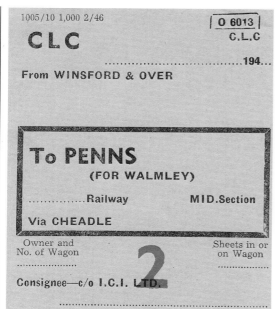

1005/10 1,000 2/46

CLC

O 6013
C.L.C

....194...

From WINSFORD & OVER

To PENNS
(FOR WALMLEY)

...............Railway   **MID.Section**

Via CHEADLE

| Owner and No. of Wagon | Sheets in or on Wagon |

2

Consignee—c/o I.C.I. LTD.

....

Freight was always the most important traffic on the branch in CLC eyes. The pre-Grouping pattern wagon label recorded a wagon load from Winsford to Irlam via Baguley in 1895. The unused post-Grouping label was printed in 1945 for use on the regular ICI traffic.
Both: David Bownes Collection

January 1891, to demand the immediate resumption of services. It was argued that the Committee had violated the Railway & Canal Traffic Act (1854), which stated that railway companies were obliged to 'afford all due and reasonable facilities' for the handling of passenger traffic on railways which had been constructed for that purpose. In his judgement Justice Wills ruled that the CLC was indeed liable under the terms of the Act to carry passengers, especially as the Winsford Branch was a profitable undertaking when passenger and goods traffic were taken together. The CLC's complaint about the financial hardship of complying with Colonel Rich's report was rejected out of hand, because the company was perceived to have incurred these expenses by 'deliberately running down the line' and by putting in unauthorised sidings. Similarly the Committee's plea that passenger traffic by itself was unprofitable was dismissed 'as completely subordinate' to the issue in the case.

Compelled to reintroduce a passenger service, the CLC determined to make the best of the situation. The recommendations of the Board of Trade were implemented at a cost of £7,514 and the line reopened for business in 1892. Services were improved with the three trains a day increased to six and through excursions were run to destinations such as New Brighton and Doncaster. The committee's efforts paid off and passenger journeys increased from 7,100 in 1886 to 99,339 in 1924. Goods traffic also continued to pay its way, although the CLC was never able

fully to exploit the salt mines it had expended so much money to serve, as it could not compete with the Weaver Navigation so far as the transportation of salt for export was concerned. The Salt Union owned large fleets of barges capable of carrying huge loads through to the docks at Liverpool and even in the post-Grouping era the amount of salt shipped from the Winsford district by rail was less than half that carried by water. So the CLC concentrated its efforts on supplying salt for the domestic market including industry, and also transported coal to the mines and general merchandise to the town. For these purposes the CLC ran a total of six goods trains a day.

For most of its working life the branch was supplied with locomotives from Northwich, which were housed at Winsford Shed. In addition the Salt Union (which represented most of the local mines) ran its own locomotives, although shunting duties were more often carried out by horses. The big salt proprietors had their own rolling stock painted in their liveries, and their own wagon repair shops at Winsford. Common salt was loaded into open wagons but the fine salt which required protection from the elements was carried in covered wagons with tent-shaped roofs to ensure good drainage.

But these better times for the branch did not last long. As recession began to bite in the late 1920s, the Winsford Branch was once again making a loss. Passenger figures slumped to a low point of 65,515 in 1927 and showed little sign of recovery. At the same time the company was compelled by the Rates Tribunal to introduce cheap tickets for workmen, the maximum fare from Winsford to Manchester and Winsford to Chester being fixed at 1s 5d and 1s 2d respectively. This compared with a third class standard fare for the same journey of 6s 8d to Manchester and 5s 0d to Chester. Not surprisingly the branch reported a greater fall in receipts (54%) following the introduction of the scheme than in passenger figures (32%), although the downward trend of both was all too apparent. To make matters worse, the goods traffic was no longer the profitable business it had once been and the amount of freight carried on the line barely covered the running costs.

In an effort to save money, one of the new Sentinel railcars (No 602) was introduced on the Winsford Branch in July 1929 and the existing engine shed closed, as Northwich assumed control of the branch rosters. To make full use of the replacement service, the number of passenger trains was increased to eight a day in each direction, with a through service to Northwich offered on Saturdays. A small saving was made and a slight increase in traffic recorded but the service was still poorly used, with an average of only 13 passengers to a train. One reason for this was the slowness of the railcar, which due to speed restrictions travelled the route at 16mph. Another and more serious reason was road competition.

The CLC was not alone in finding itself faced by this new threat, nor was the Winsford Branch the only victim. Throughout Britain the profitability of many minor routes was being eroded by the rise of road transport. The Big Four railway companies responded by securing a change in the law, which allowed them to operate an alternative service of motor vehicles in districts where competition made the cost of running passenger trains prohibitive. To exercise these powers (which came into effect in 1929), the railway companies adopted a policy of securing a financial interest in existing road omnibus companies. In the context of Cheshire the LMS and LNER had purchased 50% of the shares in the North Western Road Car Co (NWRCC) and looked to see a return on their investment through the closure of unremunerative branch lines.

Bad though this was for the Winsford Branch, the appointment of Sidney Burgoyne as the new manager of the CLC in 1929 sealed its fate. The company of which he took charge was in financial trouble. The CLC as a whole was beginning to lose money and the parent companies demanded action. Unimpressed with the marginal

Above: Handbill announcing the resumption of passenger services on the line in February 1892, following the order of the Railway & Canal Commission. It is interesting to note that apart from CLC destinations, the bill also promotes the MSLR service to Hawarden and Wrexham.
David Bownes Collection

improvements in the performance of the Winsford Branch, Burgoyne ordered the withdrawal of passenger facilities from 1 January 1931. However, in order to retain as much of the main line traffic as possible and to comply with the law, he first arranged for the NWRCC to run a bus service in substitution for that provided by rail, before announcing the closure in the local press on 28 November 1930. Furious at not having been consulted, Winsford Urban and District Council branded Burgoyne's actions 'high handed and abrupt'. Local opinion was also outraged, as it was felt that the replacement service was inferior, despite being more frequent, and could be withdrawn at any moment. In mid-December representatives from the council and local associations met Burgoyne to request a postponement pending negotiations but found the manager unshakeable in his resolve.

In a last attempt to save the service, a

CLOSING OF THE
WINSFORD BRANCH FOR PASSENGER TRAFFIC
On and from
THURSDAY, JANUARY 1st, 1931
THE PASSENGER TRAIN SERVICE
between
WINSFORD & OVER AND CUDDINGTON
WILL BE WITHDRAWN and
Winsford & Over and Whitegate Stations
will be closed for Passenger Traffic.

From that date an Omnibus Service will be provided by the North-Western Road Car Company between Winsford & Over, Whitegate and Cuddington to connect at Cuddington Station with the Rail Services run by the Cheshire Lines Railway on the Manchester-Chester line.

This road service will provide more frequent services than the existing Passenger Train Service on the Branch line.

It has been arranged that the existing half-hourly service run by the North-Western Road Car Company between Winsford & Over and Northwich Town shall be extended to serve Northwich Station, Cheshire Lines Railway.

Owners of unexpired return halves of Railway Tickets available over the Winsford Branch will be permitted to travel on their return journey within the period of availability of their tickets on the Omnibuses of the North-Western Road Car Company between Cuddington, Whitegate, and Winsford & Over.

PARCELS AND MISCELLANEOUS TRAFFIC.
Winsford & Over and Whitegate Stations will continue to deal with parcels and miscellaneous traffic, also horses, cattle, and other livestock, as at present.

GOODS, MINERAL AND LIVESTOCK TRAFFIC.
There will be no change in regard to the handling of goods, mineral and livestock traffic.

Winsford & Over and Whitegate Stations will continue to deal with these traffics as at present.

BUS SERVICE. JANUARY 1st, 1931.

WEEK DAYS.

		a.m.	a.m.	a.m.	p.m.	p.m.	p.m.	p.m.	p.m.	p.m.	p.m.	p.m.	p.m.
CUDDINGTON	dep	7 5	8 45	10 50	12 6	1 15	2 0	3 5	3 55	4 50	5 52		
WINSFORD	arr	7 28	9 8	11 13	12 25	1 38	2 23	3 28	4 18	5 13	6 15		
WINSFORD	dep	7 30	9 10	11 13	12 25	1 38	2 30	3 28	4 20	6 15	6 15		
CUDDINGTON	arr	7 53	9 33	11 35	12 50	2 0	2 53	3 50	4 43	6 38	6 35		

CUDDINGTON	dep	p.m. 7 15	p.m. 7 20	p.m. 7 25	p.m. 8 15	p.m. 9 15	p.m. 10 0	p.m. 10 50
WINSFORD	arr	7 28	7 43	7 48	8 38	9 38	10 22	11 13
WINSFORD	dep	7 28						
CUDDINGTON	arr	7 50	8 8	9 0	10 0	10 46		

SUNDAYS.

		p.m.	p.m.	p.m.	p.m.	p.m.	p.m.	p.m.	p.m.	p.m.	p.m.	p.m.
CUDDINGTON	dep	2 0	2 5	3 55	4 50	5 52	7 5	8 0	9 15	10 0		
WINSFORD	arr	2 23	3 28	4 18	5 13	6 15	7 28	8 23	9 38	10 22		
WINSFORD	dep	2 30	3 28	4 20	5 15	6 15	7 28	8 30	9 38	10 23		
CUDDINGTON	arr	2 53	3 50	4 43	5 38	6 35	7 50	9 0	10 0	10 45		

Central Station, Liverpool.   S. T. BURGOYNE, *Manager.*

Left: Official closure notice for the branch, as published in the *Northwich Guardian* on 28 November 1930. The times and routes of replacement bus services are listed. *Cheshire CC Record Office/ David Bownes Collection*

campaign was mounted to demonstrate its potential, with the result that unprecedented numbers used the railway during its final fortnight. But this belated effort made little impact on the accounts, which revealed that the branch had grossed a mere £9,370 during 1930, of which only £809 was attributable to passenger traffic. Expenditure for the same period equalled £13,477, leaving an operational loss of £4,107. Burgoyne's decision now seemed all the more justified, as it was projected to save the company over £4,200 per annum, half of which would come from redundancies at Winsford and Whitegate. Long term savings were also expected, as the reduction in trains would naturally result in less maintenance.

Unable to persuade Burgoyne to reintroduce the service, Winsford Council brought a second action against the CLC before the Court of the Railway and Canal Commission in July 1931. The nub of the Council's argument was that in withdrawing passenger facilities the CLC had disregarded and disobeyed an injunction of the court which was still in force and which the Committee had elected to abide by for 40 years. Once again it was argued that the question of loss was wholly subsidiary, as branch lines were known to have a contributive value. Besides it was contended that the public had a right to expect services as £60 million of taxpayers' money had been given to the railway

companies under the Railways Act of 1921.

However, the CLC was on much stronger ground than it had been in 1891. The new Act enabling railways companies to replace unprofitable routes with bus services was very much in the company's favour. But the real ace in the CLC's pack was the decision of the Appeal Court in a similar case, which had ruled that the 1891 order against the company had been a 'mistake in law'. The Commission agreed that in retrospect it had been beyond the jurisdiction of the court to order the resumption of passenger services on a loss-making line. Furthermore the court ruled that even if it had such jurisdiction it would not grant it in this case, because the CLC had done all in its power to make the line pay. The action was dismissed and the original order rescinded.

With passenger traffic withdrawn for the last time, the Winsford Branch settled down to life as a quiet freight line. Salt and coal traffic continued, though declining gently, and dairy produce, fruit and vegetables continued to be sent from Whitegate to destinations such as Manchester, Leeds and Birmingham. The two stations which had once employed over 20 people between them were reduced to a skeleton staff. Removing the signalling for passenger trains and replacing it with a simpler block system made further savings. The number of freight trains also declined to three a day in each direction, with two on Saturdays and none on Sundays. This latter factor enabled the branch to run occasional football specials but even these had ceased to operate by the outbreak of World War 2. In its final days under CLC ownership the branch's main traffic was with ICI, who had taken control of the old Salt Union in 1938, and with the local farms and businesses which continued to use the line for supplies.

Like so many branch lines, the Winsford Railway failed to live up to the expectations of its promoters. Its profitability was at best erratic and its contributive value as a passenger line doubtful. If it had fulfilled Watkin's expectations, the resulting growth into south Cheshire would have dramatically extended the CLC's network and ironically would have given greater credibility to the company's title than its later expansion into Lancashire was to warrant.

8

Locomotives and Rolling Stock

A fully-fledged railway company in every other respect, it might seem surprising that the Cheshire Lines Committee relied entirely on motive power supplied by the parent companies. The only exception to this state of affairs were four CLC-owned Sentinel railcars operated during the 1930s and the usual shunting and carting horses which were once such a familiar sight on Britain's railways.

Locomotives
From the earliest days of the CLC, engines were provided by the MSLR, due to the proximity of its locomotive works at Gorton, compared with those

of the Midland and Great Northern companies at Derby and Doncaster. In 1873 the mileage charge made for locomotive hire to the CLC was 11d for passenger trains and 3¼d for goods. Consequently, as a parent company, the MSLR's contribution to the cost of motive power was considerably reduced when the profit made from locomotive hire was taken into account. The Midland and Great Northern directors were never happy with this arrangement and argued from the beginning that the CLC should possess its own locomotives. Due to continual pressure from its partners in the CLC, the MSLR reduced the hire charge in 1878 to 9½d and 1¾d respectively but this was still not enough to satisfy the Midland and Great Northern directors and the matter was put to external arbitration in 1882.

The discussions were chaired by John Ramsbottom, the former Locomotive Superintendent of the LNWR and a respected authority on such matters. A number of alternatives were put forward, including a three-way provision of locomotives by each of the

Below: An official CLC photograph of an MSLR Sacré 4-4-0 (No 423, later GCR Class 6B No 423B) at Manchester Central on a Liverpool train. The tender-mounted bell and cords for the passenger alarm system are a feature of many late 19th century pictures of MS&L locomotives. *Ian Allan Library*

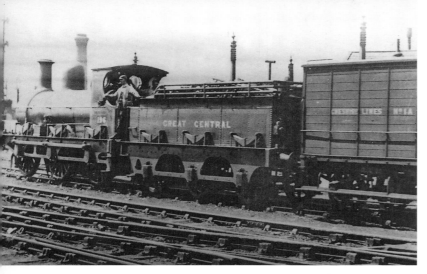

Left: GCR Class 23 0-6-0 No 196 stands in the goods yard at Manchester with a CLC brake van. The van's 'A' series number indicates that it is on the Duplicate List (as with the GCR locomotive 'B' list). Quite how the CLC, with a wagon fleet of over 3,000 but only 10 brake vans according to its 1901 statistics, should have any vans spare just a few years later, is a mystery. *Ian Allan Library/ Bucknall Collection*

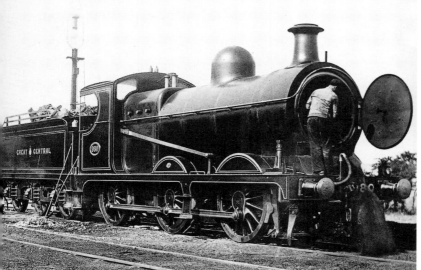

Centre left: Shovelling out the smokebox char has always been one of the less pleasant aspects of daily servicing of a steam engine. Neilson-built '9J' 0-6-0 No 980 is smartly turned out in GCR Goods livery and includes such details as the jack carried on the front footplate and the container on the tender front, which might be a jug of engine oil or equally likely a bottle of cold tea! *Ian Allan Library/ Bucknall Collection*

Below left: As on many other lines, the 4-2-2 locomotive had a brief renaissance as front-line express power on the Cheshire Lines around the turn of the century with the introduction of steam sanding. Class 13 No 971 is seen near Hough Green on a Manchester-Liverpool express *c*1911. Added to the front of the bogie stock is a 6-wheel family saloon of 1876, presumably conveying a private party who could afford something even more exclusive than first class. *Real Photographs/ GCRS Collection*

Above right: The competent Robinson 'C14' 4-4-2Ts were the mainstay of the Chester line passenger services for many years. In early BR livery, No 67430 leaves Knutsford with a Manchester Central-Northgate local on 17 August 1950. *P. M. Alexander*

Right: Special services would bring in classes of engine that the CLC was rarely privileged to see. In the 1930s, Gresley 'A1' Pacific No 2561 *Minoru* storms through Glazebrook with the annual Pullman train from King's Cross to Aintree for the Grand National, always a Pacific turn. *G. H. Platt/ E. M. Johnson Collection*

Left: A beautifully turned out 'B18' No 5195 stands on the turntable at Skelton Junction in 1939. The trackwork in the foreground is worthy of comment, as it appears that the further rail is keyed on the *inside* jaws of the chairs! *N. E. Preedy*

Below left: The demands of World War 2 brought many changes to the ordered life of the CLC, including novel motive power. WD 'Austerity' 2-10-0 No 3726 is seen at Cheadle, coupled to an unidentified LMS '4F', in August 1944. *W. Potter/Author's Collection*

Right: The other wartime 'Austerity' type, the 2-8-0, became a common sight on the CLC. No 3094 forges along with a heavy goods train near Ashley on 19 April 1947. *J. D. Darby*

parent companies. Another, favoured by the Midland and Great Northern, was for the parent companies to subscribe jointly to the cost of building new locomotives, as was the case with the M&GN and Somerset & Dorset Joint railways. However, neither option offered a real solution, as both would result in high maintenance costs being paid to the MSLR for work carried out at Gorton (the only viable location for this to be done), while the second would have been ruinously expensive for all concerned. Instead, it was ruled that engines to meet purely CLC needs were to be provided by the MSLR and that charges for both passenger and goods locomotive hire should be reduced by ¼d per mile. In addition, the MR and GNR would provide locomotives for their through trains, with the MSLR (later GCR/LNER) providing the rest of the motive power. This agreement became known as the 'Ramsbottom Award' and remained in force until nationalisation, although the mileage rates were varied over the years.

Conversely, engine sheds on the CLC were provided at the expense of the Committee but their staff, like the footplatemen, came from the MSLR and its successors. Certain sheds, such as Walton and Northwich, also stabled MR and GNR engines used on through services. In total, 16 sheds were built by the CLC, although several were relatively short lived:

CLC Engine sheds
(Opening dates are given first while only pre-1948 closing dates are included where relevant)

Allerton	1882-c1897
Birkenhead	1888
(sub-shed of Brunswick)	
Brunswick	1864
Chester	1874
(sub-shed of Northwich)	
Cornbrook	1880-1895
Heaton Mersey	1889
Helsby & Alvanley	1893-1929
(sub-shed of Northwich)	

Knutsford	c1863-c1869
Northwich	1869
Padgate	c1883-c1929
Southport	1884
(sub-shed of Walton-on-the-Hill)	
Stockport Tiviot Dale	1866-1889
Trafford Park	1894
Walton-on-the-Hill	1881
Warrington Central	opened by 1893
(sub-shed of Brunswick)	
Winsford	1870-1929
(sub-shed of Northwich)	

For the crack Liverpool to Manchester passenger services Sacré-designed 2-4-0 and 4-4-0 classes were used to begin with. Notable were the 28 locomotives of GCR Class 12A, built by the MSLR from 1875 onwards. When new they worked exclusively on the Cheshire Lines and were, in the opinion of the distinguished railway author E. L. Ahrons, writing in the *Railway Magazine*, 'one of the fastest 6 foot wheeled engines in the country.' He comments that their work between Manchester and Warrington, taking 18min for the 15¾-mile run (a speed of 52.5mph), 'was probably the smartest locomotive performance on any British railway for many years'.

These locomotives were displaced by 'Sacré Singles'. 12 Class 14 2-2-2s built in 1882-3 and all of which were working on the CLC by 1887. The first locomotives to dominate this service, they in turn gave way to another renowned single, the Pollitt Class 13 4-2-2, six of which had been built in 1900 to work the London Extension. They came as a class to the CLC, where they were concentrated on express workings. In turn supplanted by Pollitt and Parker designs of 4-4-0,

the surviving locomotives remained on secondary duties until 1927. Various classes of 4-4-0 then controlled the main line express services, with Pollitt-designed LNER Class D6 proving particularly successful. Over the years these were one of the most commonly used and best remembered passenger locomotives on the CLC.

From 1933 LNER Class D9 locomotives, the first locomotives designed by Robinson for the GCR and built between 1901 and 1904, were drafted in. By the outbreak of World War 2, six of this class of 40 engines were at Brunswick Shed and five at Trafford Park Shed. These transfers continued until 1947, by which time all the 27 survivors were on the CLC, with the class having a virtual monopoly of the hourly Liverpool to Manchester expresses, on which the extended wartime schedule of 55 minutes with two stops was still in force. Despite its by then run-down condition, this class was held in high esteem and locomotives usually managed to complete their journeys whatever the mechanical problems.

Passenger services between Manchester and Chester were largely the preserve of Sacré 2-4-0s until replaced by various 4-4-0s. LNER Class D5 took over the service when all six locomotives moved to Trafford Park Shed in 1921. They moved on to Walton Shed, Liverpool, to be used at the sub-shed at Southport and allow LNER Class E2 and its 4-4-0 development LNER 'D8' to be sent for scrap in 1926. Replacing them on the Manchester to Chester service were LNER Class D7, six of which were shedded at Northwich between 1921 and 1930. These locomotives were in turn replaced by LNER Class C13 4-4-2Ts, which ran the service for many years, although a single Class C14 4-4-2T (No 6212) was allocated

to Northwich in 1937 and worked the Chester line until transferred to Colwick in early 1940.

Whereas the solitary Ivatt 4-4-2T was much disliked and considered underpowered by CLC engine men, the Robinson 4-4-2Ts based at Trafford Park were one of his most successful designs and valued for both local and express passenger workings. Quite capable of keeping time on the Liverpool to Manchester express service if called upon to do so, they also worked local trains around Manchester including those to Irlam.

During the early years, goods traffic was most commonly hauled by Sacré-designed 0-6-0s, with examples of Classes 6C, 18, 18A and 23 being recorded at Stockport Shed in 1886. The Class 18 single-framed tender version was originally designed with the CLC in mind and the equivalent tank engine Class 18T, built from 1880 onwards, was allocated to the Liverpool North Extension Line. Sacré-designed LNER Class J12 0-6-0s were in general use on heavy goods and occasional excursion work from 1880 to 1930, although inter-war goods services were dominated by LNER Class J9 and J10 locomotives.

'J10s' were quite capable of coping with such passenger services as the Manchester to Chester trains and football specials between Manchester Central and Manchester United football ground. LNER Class J11 was the first new goods engine to be designed by Robinson and built 1901-1910. They were firm favourites with engine crews and worked nearly every class of train from pick-up goods to express passenger when required to do so. Nearly every CLC shed had some of the 174-strong class at some time. Together with Class J9 and J10, they earned a reputation as the steam workhorses of the CLC.

It should be noted, however, that for many years most of the shunting duties continued to be carried out by horses, and in common with locomotives these were originally supplied to the CLC by the MSLR. From November 1909 the purchase of horses for use on the CLC was undertaken by each of the parent companies in turn for a period of 12 months, the maximum price for a 'heavy shunting horse' being fixed at £83. The Committee's growing stable was managed by the horse superintendent, who worked out of Liverpool Central. As with other railway companies, considerable pride was shown in these workhorses and competitions for the best turned out were held regularly.

The post-Grouping era witnessed the introduction of ex-GNR and MR designs to assist with internal services and for a time the 'C1'

Atlantics were regular performers on the Liverpool line. However, ex-GCR engines continued to predominate, among the most active being LNER Classes B7, B9, C12, C13, D6, D9, F1, F2, J11, J39, N5 and O4. LMS engines seen on the CLC during this period included 0-6-0 Classes 3F and 4F, and 2-6-2T and 4-4-0 types, as well as the powerful Class 8 locomotives used to haul limestone trains from the Peak District to ICI's Northwich plant.

By virtue of the through trains which ran onto its network, it is arguable that the CLC over the years had on its metals a greater variety of locomotives than any other joint line or indeed any other 143 route miles of track. As well as regular services, the boat trains, excursion trains, race trains and special trains brought the more unusual types. Locomotives running in after construction or overhaul at Gorton and Derby would visit Manchester Central and perhaps work the Liverpool service. Manchester Central was the chosen venue for special events such as the visit of the restored Great Northern Single and the newly constructed 'A4' *Sir Nigel Gresley* when they were displayed to promote the LNER in the 1930s. The range is wide and it would be fascinating to try and list them all but many appear in the photographs. It has been postulated before that a probable reason why so few photographs were taken on the CLC was because locomotives used on the railway were more easily seen elsewhere. In the early days of railway photography the locomotive was considered the main subject and only latterly did the whole railway scene become attractive.

The CLC's sole contribution to motive power came about as the result of the economic crisis experienced during the late 1920s. A combination of falling receipts and pressure for an improvement from the LMS, led the CLC to accept a tender from Messrs Cammell-Laird in January 1929 for four Sentinel-Cammell railcars delivered during that year. These were projected to effect an annual saving of £4,465. Their total cost was put at £15,166, while running costs were estimated to be 11¼d a mile, 9½d cheaper than conventional traction. Numbered 600-3, the railcars were originally finished in CLC teak livery but were later painted buff & brown. They saw active service on most of the network, including the Winsford Branch and the section between Altrincham and Stockport. At one stage they were all shedded at Brunswick and worked out of Southport, Widnes and Warrington. Problems were experienced with the railcars from their introduction and all four were scrapped in 1944, three of them having been in store at Trafford Park since November 1941.

Despite making good commercial sense for the parent companies, the virtual monopoly in locomotive supply enjoyed by the MSLR and its successors did not necessarily serve the best interests of the Cheshire Lines. According to A. J. Pearson (an officer of the CLC during the 1920s), 'the CL people were not always satisfied with the quality of the locomotives supplied to them under [the 1882] arrangement, and often there were complaints'. The reason for this stemmed from the MSLR/GCR practice of retiring certain classes of engine to the CLC once they had been supplanted on heavier duties. Indeed, Vinson Gulliver, an ex-fireman, recalled that the GCR seemed reluctant to scrap anything so long as they could make use of it elsewhere.

Obviously, the use of antiquated locomotives militated against the CLC's claims of being a 'modern' railway company, and engine failures figure heavily in the early years of the company's minutes. Unfortunately for the CLC, this practice continued into LNER days. For example, by the time of nationalisation, Northwich Shed did not contain a single locomotive built by the LNER, the most modern being Class L1 No 9062 (used for banking duties at Winnington) which was built by the GCR in 1917, while the average age of the other locomotives stabled there was 46 years. Similarly, all of the 26 surviving 'D9' 4-4-0s were operating on the CLC in 1948, as were 76 of the remaining 77 'J10' 4-4-0s. On the whole, however, engines ascribed to the Committee performed well, due to the relatively less demanding work asked of them on the joint line, and several early designs could be said to have served an honourable retirement away from their original stamping grounds.

Rolling Stock

The first coaches used on the four small companies which became the CLC were provided by the MSLR and GN jointly, as were the coaches on the Garston to Brunswick line opened on 1 June 1864. In February 1864 it was decided that the GN and MSLR should find stock in equal proportions, again at a mileage rate: a halfpenny a mile for first and composite carriages, two fifths of a penny for all other carriage stock, a third of a penny for wagons and one twelfth of a penny for wagon sheets.

But on 23 June 1864 the Officers' meeting recommended to the Committee that a separate stock of carriages should be provided for working the traffic on the Joint Lines. Matters moved swiftly and tenders were invited for eight types of vehicle to drawings provided by Mr Sacré, locomotive engineer of the MSLR. Orders were placed on 1 March 1865 with the Metropolitan

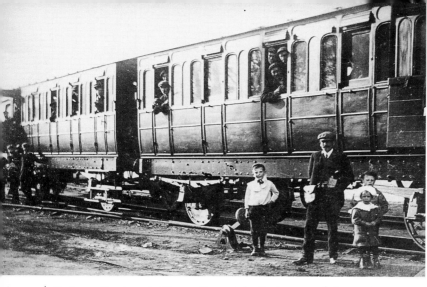

Railway Carriage & Wagon Co and the Railway Carriage Co of Oldbury. All four-wheeled, the prices ranged from £390 for first class carriages to £198 10s for horseboxes; a total of 47 were ordered, with three carriage trucks provided by the parent companies.

As new lines were opened, further vehicles were ordered in 1873 from the Metropolitan Railway Carriage & Wagon Co, the Ashbury Railway Carriage & Iron Co and the MSLR. Still all four-wheeled, the passenger carriages remained to MSLR designs while the horseboxes followed Great Northern practice. A recommendation to order 'six first class and six second class carriages of the kind suggested by Mr Pullman' was deferred and not heard of again. However, when the line from Southport opened in 1885, there was brief use of a Pullman parlour car as a through coach to London, which suggests that the idea lingered on. In December 1875, on the report of the manager that the LNWR was using cushioned third class carriages on its trains between Manchester London Road and Liverpool, the officers agreed to recommend that CLC carriages should also be cushioned. Owing to other companies also fitting up their third class carriages, the cost of this action was found to have risen to £27 0s 4d per carriage.

In preparation for the opening of the new Manchester Central station in 1880, Gorton Shops had started work on new stock for the planned 'pendulum service' of half-hourly trains to Liverpool. This was to be operated by the MSLR for the first 18 months and Watkin planned to do it in style. However, his colleagues would agree to only an hourly service and, despite the objection of Mr Sacré, the coaches were sold to the CLC. As the coaches represented the last word in contemporary MSLR practice, Sacré had wanted

his railway to get some credit for the service to Liverpool Central, which was then commonly called the Midland station. Despite bogie carriages being considered, the 62 new stock were six-wheeled and, because of public preference at the time, were compartmented.

Such was the importance of the Manchester to Liverpool service, that longer and even more luxurious carriages were considered for the expresses. In 1878 the Ashbury Co agreed to build four bogie coaches with 12 wheels at £950 each. Further orders followed at higher prices in 1880. The last of these carriages were not condemned until 1931.

Goods trucks were ordered intermittently and as required.

The next major order for carriages was placed with Craven Bros prior to the opening of the Aintree to Southport line in September 1884. Again these were 12-wheeled carriages — 28 in all but with a higher proportion of third class. In 1887 the next order for carriages from Cravens was for 53 'modern type' six-wheeled carriages to replace the 1865 stock. Only first and third class compartments were specified. The last second class carriages, seven six-wheelers of five compartments each, were ordered from Cravens in August 1888 and second class was abolished on the CLC from 1 January 1892.

Automatic vacuum brakes were fitted to new orders of stock from 1889 and conversion of chosen passenger vehicles started in 1890. The same year and despite earlier experiments with Stone electric lighting, the decision was taken to light carriages with compressed oil gas. Progress on conversion was rapid and 303 carriages had been so fitted by June 1892.

The next 10 years saw a replacement programme of old six-wheel coaches by modern

Above: A newly-built CLC non-corridor composite coach at Doncaster Works in the 1900s. The first class compartments, and one third class, have access to lavatories. The CLC crest was normally carried only on first class and composite stock, not all-thirds, and became increasingly rare during the Grouping years.
National Railway Museum

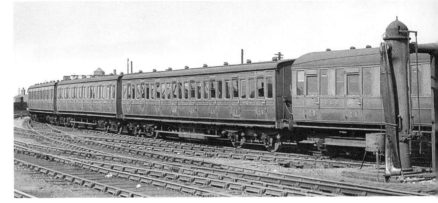

Upper right: A rake of CLC non-corridor stock of earlier years stands at Manchester Central on 25 July 1949. Such stock was typical of many services at the time. *P. Ward*

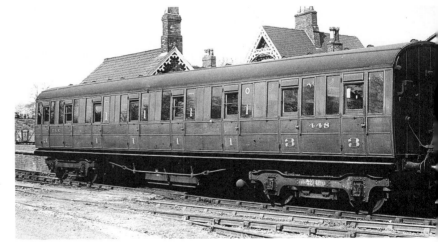

Centre right: A Doncaster built non-corridor composite on Gresley type bogies is seen in the bay road at Baguley on 15 April 1949. *J. D. Darby*

Below right: 'Austerity' Class J94 0-6-0ST No 68012 shunts stock headed by CLC 15-ton brake van No 3610 at Manchester Central in July 1949.
P. Ward

Left: Freight consignments from the docks in the region demanded specialised goods vehicles. This is a 10-ton refrigerated meat van in CLC livery. *Historical Model Railway Society Collection*

ones to MSLR design, though manufactured by outside firms, adding Brown Marshall & Co to those mentioned above. Some four-wheel bogie carriages were ordered in 1896, partly to replace the previously requested six-wheelers. The extension of rolling stock ceased in 1897 and the total number of carriages remained at 447 until 1926, though the pace of renewal did not slacken, with older vehicles being relegated to the duplicate list. By now typical prices at which tenders were accepted were: four bogie composites from Lancaster Railway Carriage & Wagon Co at £2,145 each, and from the Metropolitan Railway Carriage & Wagon Co, four bogie third brakes at £1,711 each. These examples were twelve-wheelers, with the new elliptical roof recently adopted by the Great Central Railway for its new stock for the London service, and they had other details to match including lavatory accommodation. As far as coach lighting was concerned, by the publication of the 28 March 1898 Appendix to the Working Timetable, the CLC was able to state that all its stock had been fitted with appliances for lighting with gas and filling stations were at Liverpool Central, Brunswick and Manchester Central.

On 2 April 1901 it was agreed that Mr Parker 'be put on the same basis as the superintendent of the parent companies', with the sole responsibility for keeping the Committee's stock in proper condition in respect of both renewals and repairs. Horseboxes, carriage trucks and milk trucks were the first to be renewed in a programme lasting until 1906. In 1903 it became clear that further replacement of old coaches was necessary and in 1904 and 1905 tenders were accepted to replace six-wheel coaches with a

similar number of four-wheel bogie carriages: 32 carriages were ordered in all from a number of outside suppliers, with the Brush Electric & Engineering Co now joining the list.

The GCR was building a new carriage and wagon works at Dukinfield, and to ease pressure of work at Gorton pending the new works' completion, it was agreed that a number of carriages should be repaired at Doncaster and Derby. When outside tenders were invited for further new stock in 1908, prices quoted to the CLC were so high that orders were placed instead with the Midland for two bogie third brakes at £1,080 each and two bogie saloons at £1,175 each, and with the Great Northern for six horseboxes at £281 4s 0d each and 10 refrigerated meat vans at £207 10s 0d each. The Midland supplied carriages to its normal style but rather than paint and grain, it built the bodies in teak at extra cost to itself. The horseboxes were generally to Great Northern detail, while the refrigerated meat vans were purely to its design.

In July 1910 the Carriage & Wagon Superintendent drew the Board's attention to the fact that the carriages of the duplicate stock averaged 32¾ years in age, with a large number four- and six-wheeled. He recommended the provision of 'two or three trains of modern, up to date bogie carriages to run the Manchester and Liverpool services, where competition is so keen, and thus liberate some of the present stock for working in suburban trains'. As a result, the parent companies were invited to tender for '45 modern bogie carriages' and in February 1914 the GCR began to build at Dukinfield, with deliveries the same year.

No more renewals took place until World

War 1 was over, when recommendations were made that two new five-coach trains be provided for the express service and that a number of six-wheeled vehicles be formed into close-coupled trains and fitted with electric lighting. The six-wheeled coaches were dealt with first, though electric lighting was not fitted, and by 1921 10 trains had been delivered. The new trains for the express service took longer to approve, despite several requests by Mr Robinson, but in 1923 a tender from Cravens was accepted for both the new trains and additional carriages, bringing the total number purchased to 32. Prices ranged from eight bogie firsts at £3,730 each to 18 bogie thirds at £2,990 each. Like all new CLC carriages, they were finished in varnished teak, having a very elaborate painting specification .with transfer arms and 3in long yellow block letters and numerals blocked light and dark blue, shaded black splashed white. Old coaches were always painted oak brown and also carried the CLC crest.

Further renewal orders were given to Cravens in 1925. In 1927 the Board approved a recommendation by the parent companies that 'the stock appearing in the published accounts of the Committee at 31 December 1922 including duplicates, shall be taken as the standard of Cheshire Line Stock'. From that time, future orders for carriages and wagons on the renewal account were supposed to be entirely dependent on the number of vehicles broken up. In fact, such was the state of many of the old carriages that the scrapping proceeded at some speed and in excess of the number required for renewals to be authorised or even necessary.

In 1928 Cravens and LNER Dukinfield Works supplied new carriages to meet renewal requirements but later that year the Board decided to purchase modern type bogie carriages from the parent companies in ownership proportion. The LMS sent four in 1930 — which had been built at Wolverton in 1898, 1901 and 1904 respectively. The LNER sent four built in 1927 by Hurst, Nelson & Co for the North Eastern section but also two built by the NER in 1906. Obviously, given the chance, it was not only old locomotives that were sent to end their years on the CLC. When the MSJAR was electrified in 1931 its stock of steam-hauled bogie carriages was purchased by the CLC, which meant that six-wheeled coaches on local services could finally be replaced.

The last new coaches for the CLC were again built by Cravens and delivered in 1937. These were to designs by Nigel (later Sir Nigel) Gresley and to basically standard LNER pattern. Apart from one isolated open third, these consisted of three trains each of eight coaches of articulated stock, which as state-of-the-art passenger rolling stock ran on the Liverpool to Manchester service and continued the tradition that the newest and best trains were used on the 'City Links City' line. The only further rolling stock purchases were a few goods brake vans from the LNER in 1939 and 1940.

Effectively, from the end of the 1920s the quantity of rolling stock on the CLC had begun to decline. The majority of goods vehicles were pooled into LNER and LMS stock in 1930, leaving only 43 brake vans and 35 utility types owned by the Committee. Carriages, which had stayed at a consistent number for many years, declined sharply, so that at the outbreak of war only 284 (211 uniform class and 73 composite) remained with the CLC.

9

Stations and Signalling

The catchwords for the CLC for someone who knew it well are probably variety, diversity and even occasionally eccentricity. Nowhere is this better demonstrated than in its station buildings, which ranged from major metropolitan termini such as Manchester Central and Liverpool Central, through to the most bucolic of country stations such as Delamere and Cheadle. Hard to believe now but Cheadle was once what as children we called 'real' country and not subsumed by urban sprawl and entangled in motorways. In between the major stations and the small wayside ones come others that are hardly less important to the locations they serve. Again they demonstrate variety both in place and style.

Southport, a fashionable seaside resort, demanded and got a station appropriate to Lord Street, a major area for upmarket shopping. Stringent conditions were applied by the Council, resulting in a fine station which caused the LYR to rebuild its own station to remain competitive. Chester, the county town, had to be content with a plain brick-built shed covering two platforms, quite put in the shade by Thompson's magnificent Chester General station nearby. Warrington Central, the principal non-terminal station on the CLC, was built of yellow brick with stone dressings. The long, one-storey frontage of 20 bays had Italianate, roundheaded, rusticated openings, some single and some coupled with

patterned glazing bars. In the centre stood a giant triangular pediment flanked by short balustraded parapets, solid further on and with a large pitch porte-cochére. At the east end a solitary terminal block with an ornamental dormer and a French pavilion roof lacked any balancing counterpart. Impressive though the frontage was, it was noticed by very few passengers, as most favoured the more convenient stairs down to Horse Market Street.

Northwich was rebuilt in yellow brick in 1897. It had much false gabling over an intricately patterned iron canopy. As one of the busiest stations on the line, it suffered from a curiously incompleted look, caused because the LNWR, who shared the station, refused to pay to have its platform and offices improved to match the standard of the CLC. Stockport Tiviot Dale was designed by Mr Magnall, a Manchester architect, and built at the cost of about £8,000 in 1865. Variously described as Italianate or ecclesiastical in style, it had a continuously arcaded frontage with a total of 30 bays. The main feature externally was a Dutch gabled centre section with a projecting seven-arch arcade. Internally, having entered in the centre and passed the booking office, passengers found refreshment rooms on the left and an attractive and unusual wrought-iron lattice footbridge. This had a span of just over 60 feet and a sloping floor without steps, which could disconcert the unwary traveller. There was an overall roof at the east end of the down side of the station, which covered the bay platforms used for a time by the Woodley service.

The intermediate stations built at the time that their particular stretch of line was completed tend to show the style of the then parent. So the earliest stations, those on the Stockport & Altrincham Junction, are very much of the MSLR with only traces of Great Northern influence. Cheadle, Northenden and Baguley are built as one- and two-storey brick pavilions with a single-storey section between. The steep roof was brought forward on iron columns with shallow curved brackets to make a waiting shelter. A small waiting shelter, the side shed, stood on the opposite platform. In later years these were often covered in (as were the ones on the Manchester to Liverpool main line) and had fireplaces with

Above left: Delamere station in June 1951 has the atmosphere of a CLC station in early BR days before the LMR influence began to intrude. The buildings, platform faces and bridge, of local stone, are typical of much Chester line architecture. The old coach serving as a bicycle store is on the right. The tall signal posts, one with co-acting arms, are placed to give best visibility to footplate crews. *Oliver Carter*

Left: Very few pictures exist of the CLC signalling works at Warrington Battersby Lane; this 1961 view shows the hydraulic tower that fed the works. Curiously the lamp on the extreme right is on a platform-style post rather then the plain lamp posts normally used in yards.
Peter Norton/Author's Collection

chimneys fitted. Despite the fact that the Midland became a formal partner in the CLC only in 1866, the year the stations were built, the barge-boarding can be said to be Midland inspired.

This is even more the case on the new Manchester to Liverpool main line, where similar station buildings were standard but with even more ornate barge-boarding, often differing in pattern on the same building. Bay windows were absent in these later stations and doors and window openings were debased Gothic in coloured brick. Typical examples, all built in 1873, were Sankey, Widnes North and Hough Green. Irlam had an unusual covered awning, made necessary by the fact that the building of the Manchester Ship Canal altered the position of the line and required a new station to be provided. When this station had been built, the position of the line was again altered and wide platforms, together with awnings to link to the station building, were needed. Urmston was notable for its heavy commuter traffic and so provided ample protection above its platforms.

The line to Chester, built by the Cheshire Midland and the West Cheshire, had an individual cottage style station built of brick in the case of the former and red sandstone the latter. Delamere and Mouldsworth were excellent and attractive examples of those built in stone while Plumbley and Mobberley were typical of those built in

brick. Barrow for Tarvin on the other hand was built by the CLC at the same time as the main line from Manchester to Liverpool and was an identical design to those MSLR-inspired stations. Knutsford, the town that Mrs Elizabeth Gaskell used as her model for Cranford in the book of the same name, had a station with a more imposing style, though again built of brick. It also had a circular water tower with a brick-built base which, though found elsewhere on British railways, was unique for the CLC.

The Southport line showed its background of independence and shortage of funds in its mixture of stations, mostly cheaply built out of wood or brick. Altcar and Hillhouse had the same design as Sefton and Maghull, and these were probably two of the best examples.

Stations close to Liverpool on the main line had architecture to suit the affluent areas through which the line passed. Cressington & Grassendale station had half-hipped gable roofs together with perforated eaves, valancing and various other trimmings, which gave it a suitable special air for the two private estates whose names it took. St James, which was on the edge of an inner Liverpool residential district, still fashionable and essentially Georgian when the station was built, had a special side-bay arcaded frontage in rusticated ashlar. Garston was another fine example with much elaborate detail, including

Above left: Chorlton-cum-Hardy had an interesting history in the years when the CLC and its related lines were developing. Long after it had settled in its role as the junction where the incoming MSLR and MR lines met the CLC, 'Pom Pom' No 65179 rolls southwards into the station on a coal train in 1951. The neat goods shed had a covered loading bay, typical of a moderately busy suburban station yard. Chorlton Station Signalbox is behind the tender; the starting signal has a concrete post of the type commonly used for replacements on the CLC from the 1930s onwards. *Author*

Above: The 9.30am Liverpool-Manchester fast passes through Padgate on 17 October 1953, headed by 'Black Five' No 45239. The train's consist, mainly of ex-LNER stock in carmine & cream, includes through coaches and a restaurant car to Hull Paragon. (This is one of the photographer's favourite pictures.) *E. D. Bruton*

stone crow-stepped gables, iron cresting and stone mullions throughout, and four flights of iron-banistered stairs around a square well, with an open raftered roof with central finial and white tiled walls within.

The stations on the North Liverpool line were a mixed bunch. Some like Clubmoor were meanly constructed, and looked more temporary than permanent, whereas others were far better.

Gateacre for Woolton was built of wood, since it was on an embankment, and was the only other CLC station with an awning like Irlam. West Derby was a fine brick-built station building straddling a cutting.

The Manchester South District line had its stations designed in the style of the MSLR. However, before it was built it was transferred to the Midland Railway, which stamped its style on the stations in building them. But then the MSLR extended its line from Fairfield to join the Midland at Chorlton Junction and it became appropriate to transfer the line from Chorlton Junction to Throstle Nest Junction back to the CLC. In the process Chorlton-cum-Hardy station returned to the CLC but now with Midland features. Yet another example of how variety was produced amongst CLC stations.

Those of us fortunate enough or indeed old enough to remember the CLC, if invited to imagine a typical CLC station, might think of the cavernous and smoky terminals that were Manchester and Liverpool. We might, on the other hand, transport our imagination to a busy through station such as Northwich or Warrington. But it is most likely that we would take our thoughts back to a quiet country station. It might be built of brick or local stone and it would have a side shed on the opposite platform to the main station building. Rustic seats with ironwork

Left: A view from the road bridge of the platform ends at Cheadle in 1951 shows not only the signalling and siding arrangements but also the waiting shelter and the adjoining garden. *Author*

Right: 'Black Five' No 45103 passes Baguley signalbox on a Godley-Northwich van train in 1964. *Author*

manufactured by Heavyside in Derby would be on the platform, together with typical lamps, originally oil and in some cases converted to gas. There would be a goods shed and a few sidings, with possibly a crane and a loading gauge. But there would definitely be a typical signalbox and signals.

At the beginning of this chapter the word 'eccentric' was used in connection with the CLC. This was unkind; perhaps unique, distinctive or even idiosyncratic might be better. And these words apply to the signalling of the CLC to an even greater extent than to the stations. It is for its signalling that many enthusiasts remember the CLC best.

The CLC did not have a special signalling engineer but it was one of the duties covered by the General Engineer. So from 1863 to 1865 Wilkinson was in charge and from 1866 to 1874 Sacré, the MSLR Chief Mechanical Engineer. He was followed in 1875 by William George Scott, who held the job until 1902 and set up the signalling works at Warrington in 1883/4. From that point the CLC was independent as far as the manufacture of signalling equipment was concerned, although it continued to buy in its box equipment. On 1 October 1936 the Signalling Department was taken over by the LMS and from then on it followed that company's practice.

In 1870 the CLC decided to adopt the block system generally, with construction work being carried out at Gorton. In 1871 Stevens & Sons won the contract for signalling, though the CLC minutes do not state the locations nor the time scale required. By 1872 block working was in force between Godley and Deansgate/Broadheath Junctions and between Garston and Brunswick. Tappet locking was introduced in 1873 and standardised from then on. In this decision the

CLC was ahead of some major railway companies which did not fully install this system until the early 1900s.

Stevens & Sons signalled the new main line from Manchester to Liverpool in 1873. Baguley signalbox with its brick base was also a Stevens design. It had curved tops to the windows and was erected in 1875, which was when the Skelton to Stockport line was resignalled, and this was done by Stevens throughout. There were a small Stevens boxes at Helsby and Padgate, built in 1883, with 'flowing' barge boards. There were two Stevens signalboxes with horizontal rather than vertical boarding and these were the Hunt's Cross East box and Knutsford East box.

According to a minute of 16 September 1880, Aaron Haughton's tender for workshops and stores at Warrington was accepted, as it was the cheapest at £14,300. By 1881 these workshops were in use at Battersby Lane, Warrington, and from then on became the signal works for the CLC. Soon after, in 1883, the CLC started to build its own signalboxes and Delamere was installed in 1885. As far as paint is concerned, the dark colour was a medium to dark brown and the light colour was similar to Great Western Railway stone. Liverpool Central had a large version of the first type of CLC box, with the prominent horizontal beam below the windows and an overhang to the roof.

On the Southport Extension line built in 1884, Railway Signal Co of Liverpool equipment was used. This had tappet locking identical to the installations built for other railways. Manchester Central Cabin B was the largest on the system and was either extended or newly built in 1892, after it was demolished by a runaway Midland Railway train. The Saxby & Farmer type A box is found only in the North of England. There was an

example at Hale station and another at Northwich East and both were built around 1876.

Chorlton Junction signalbox was a Midland design, acquired by the CLC in 1891 when the line from Fallowfield was opened. In accordance with CLC practice it had roof lights added, a CLC lavatory cubicle, a CLC nameboard and other changes. Inside it had a similar mixture of block instruments. Incidentally it was an unusual feature of CLC boxes that, whatever their type, they all had skylights in the roof at the back.

Type 1B, as exemplified by Mouldsworth signalbox, ran from 1883 to 1889 and most of Type 1A were built between 1889 and 1903. Between 1903 and 1913 these were replaced by a Great Central Railway type of box, classified 2A. A variant with deeper windows was installed at Otterspool and Plumbley West around 1909, these being the only two such examples. Glazebrook West was a tall box with a brick base. Box Type 2C lacked windows in the gable end and had concrete lintels in the lower windows. An example was built at Bredbury as late as June 1932. Only two versions of this box were all timber, namely Bewsey and Heaton Mersey.

The panels used to manufacture the signalboxes were 5ft, 5ft 9in and 6ft 6in across. These were the standard sizes and were never mixed. The corner posts varied from 9in to 10in square for a small box, to 12in to 13in square on a large box.

As examples, Skelton Junction was made up of four 6ft 6in panels and West Timperley had two and a half 5ft panels, while Throstle Nest, a large box, had six 6ft panels.

The last signalbox built by the CLC was at Manchester Central, as part of an electric scheme installed by the General Railway Signalling Co. The box was a unique design, presumably inspired by the CLC, as the CLC resident engineer of the time, Mr K. C. Marian and his staff, were given the credit for the design and supervision of the work. Subcontractors for the cables were Callender's Cable & Construction Co, while the switch gear for the main power supply, together with the whole of the standby plant, was provided by the General Electric Co. The new signalbox was placed to give an excellent view of the yard in all directions, with observation platforms at both ends of the gantry. To maintain easy communication with the ground staff, loud-speaking telephones were installed.

After the LMS took over signalling in 1936, new boxes were built at Risley East and Risley West, and there was also a version of the standard design at Glazebrook East Junction. At some boxes such as Partington Junction, brick bases were put outside the wooden panels in World War 2 to provide protection from bomb blasts. However, by then the Warrington Signal Works had been closed following the takeover of

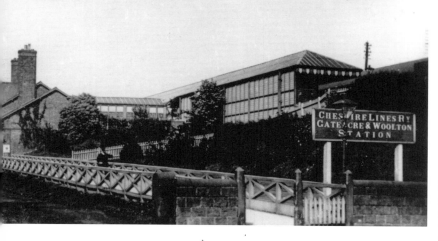

Three views of Gateacre station, showing the elaborate woodwork and two-colour canopy valance paintwork of the platform structures; also the unusual covered way leading to the platforms from the main building at the side of the embankment. *All: Lens of Sutton*

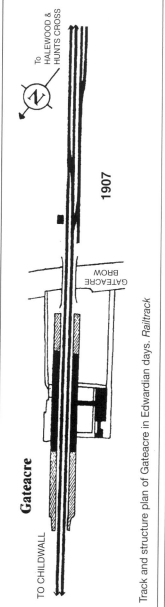

Track and structure plan of Gateacre in Edwardian days. *Railtrack*

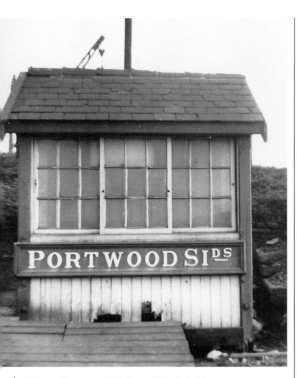

Above: Portwood Sidings Signal Cabin, near Stockport, looking very neglected towards the end of its life. *Prof Richard Challis*

Above right: The substantial Padgate Signalbox was a typical CLC box built from standard prefabricated components. Photographed in 1953. *E. D. Bruton*

signalling by the LMS. The train control centre, which had been established in 1930 in Liverpool, was modernised in 1944.

For ground cabins the CLC had two standard types. In one style the roof came down to the top of the front windows; in the other style there was approximately 2ft of boarding above the windows before the roof began.

Before 1873 the CLC followed normal Manchester, Sheffield & Lincolnshire practice for its signals. As with the signalboxes, a Stevens design was used but in 1892 the CLC adopted a special two-spectacle version of its own. The division between the equally sized red and green glasses on the signal was horizontal and in line with the centre of the arm. This was a unique feature among British railways, as was the signal finial, which comprised a closed ball and tall spike on either a square or oblong base, usually embossed with the initials of the company.

In April 1888 the first Appendix to the Working Timetables was issued and these continued until 1935. In 1892 a start was made to follow the example of the Midland and the Manchester, Sheffield & Lincolnshire railways in the change of signal lights, dispensing with white as the fixed light, using instead red for danger and green for clear. This exercise started in the Liverpool area and finished in April 1893 with the alterations to signal lights in the Chester area. During 1892/3 a complete new survey of the estate and railway tracks was carried out and in June 1907 all line distances were remeasured. The point taken as the start was from Liverpool, except for the Chester line which was measured from Manchester.

In 1908 the CLC began to remove distant signals in certain locations. The old style of distant arm was red with a straight white line. This continued until 1909 and yellow came into use as the colour of the arm in the 1920s. It had been the practice of the CLC to use rings on the signals to indicate the secondary route. In July 1916 removal of these rings from all signals that applied to goods lines began. By the time of the Grouping the final examples were removed, as by then it had become a practice that was much frowned upon generally.

The CLC adopted concrete posts at the end of World War 1 due to a shortage of timber.

Unusually, they were solid and rectangular, while wooden posts were square. This meant that they needed a special finial and at the same time the signal lamp was also to a special design. At this time concrete was also used for items of station furniture, such as nameboards.

Until the Grouping in 1923 most junction arms were at the same height with no precedence given to the more important lines, which on other railways would always be on a higher post. The Board of Trade were unhappy about this practice but the CLC was reluctant to change it, always using a separate post where possible. Tower signals was the name given to signals with a common landing and there was a magnificent display at Heaton Mersey. The well known 'Baguley Twins' were Stevens lattice signals on opposite sides of the line and with arms on both sides of the posts. The CLC used bracket signals only when it was forced to. There were early brackets at Manchester Central station and they were also used elsewhere for sighting purposes, as well as on viaducts.

Upper quadrant signals were introduced in 1929 and these needed a new design of arm. Contrary to the impression given by photographs, they were not simply the old lower quadrant arm turned upside down. Strangely, the upper quadrant signal pulled off at a lazy angle compared to the lower quadrant one.

Gantries were not common on the CLC. There were two at Manchester Central, where there was no room for spectacles, so these were put on the other side with the arms and the balance weights in the usual place. The same arrangement was also used on a gantry of signals at old Trafford Park. No cranks were used on the CLC wire runs and all were done with wheels and chains.

Early ground signals were point indicators. Later ones had their proper function but there was never more than a double version manufactured. The ground signals used the same lamps as the semaphore signals and they were identical in size. The Welch Lamp Co made them.

The CLC lever frame was based on the Stevens frame. Scott took two patents out himself but the principles were close. Lever frames were made at Warrington Works and were more substantial than the Stevens frame. A large brass plate was put on the frame, worded 'CLC Warrington Works' with the date of manufacture. It is believed that there was also a signalling school at Warrington, which used a wooden scale model of the levers and frame to train signalman.

The CLC had separate instruments for the up and down line and for sending and receiving

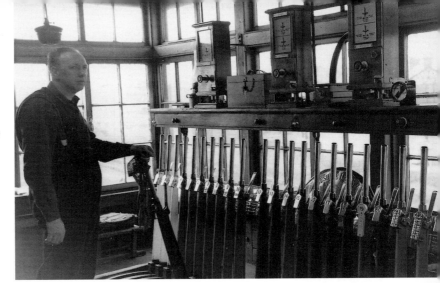

Left: Though also constructed from standard components, Cuddington Signalbox shows many design differences from Padgate. Other features of interest include the very unusual goods shed with its double loading canopies, the yard crane and the lantern for the footway in front of the signalbox.
E. D. Bruton

Upper right: Inside one of the Chester area signalboxes, with signalman Doug Haswell at the frame. Instruments and box equipment are typical of CLC practice. Behind the frame can be seen the large polished plate declaring that this was an installation of Cheshire Lines manufacture. *John E. Field*

Lower right: Reflecting its importance, Manchester Central was resignalled as a modern, electric installation in the 1930s. This 1950s view shows the main console undergoing a major maintenance and rewire operation. Despite the apparently casual look of the job, railway safety in the area would depend on 100% accuracy and precision.
British Railways

instructions. A unique feature of CLC block instruments was a little trigger to fix the reading, which could be pushed in and then pulled out to release. Otherwise the cased block instrument style was very similar to the CLC's three owning railway companies.

The first colour-light signals were installed at Brunswick in 1934 and in 1937 an NX panel was installed as part of the new signalling arrangements. This was the first one used in Britain and the forerunner of the panel signal box. It used North American technology to set a simple route, in a particularly difficult location where the main line into Liverpool Central passed Brunswick Locomotive Shed. A 3ft 6in long by 1ft high black painted panel in the signal box, was used to set the route. The signalman operated a rotary key at the first point (eNtrance) and a button at the second point of the desired route (eXit) and, if the route was clear, the points immediately took up the desired position if not already in them. The signals then indicated 'proceed'. It was thus necessary for the signalman only to know the beginning and the end of the train movement and the direction of running, in order to set up the route and clear the signals.

The CLC scheme was, as the *Railway Gazette* put it, 'prepared to meet the requirements of Mr G. Leedham, Manager and Secretary of the Cheshire Lines, by Mr K. C. Marian, Resident Engineer'. The work was carried out by the General Railway Signal Co and makes a fitting finale to signalling practice on the CLC.

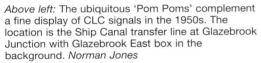

Above left: The ubiquitous 'Pom Poms' complement a fine display of CLC signals in the 1950s. The location is the Ship Canal transfer line at Glazebrook Junction with Glazebrook East box in the background. *Norman Jones*

Left: A Stevens lattice post has also been re-equipped with upper quadrant arms on the Cheadle LNWR-Northenden Junction link line. *Author*

Above: Study of signals at the Manchester end of Northwich station in August 1959. Beyond the concrete post in the foreground are some particularly fine, tall brackets. *A. Swain*

Above right: An elaborate and well-stayed bracket at Glazebrook East Junction, right by the Liverpool area boundary post. The upper quadrant fittings and concrete main post with older parts above suggest that this was a like-for-like replacement of an older bracket. *Peter Norton*

Right: CLC signal at Southport Junction, Aintree, on 6 June 1959. On a concrete post it displays an upper quadrant home arm and a lower quadrant distant. The latter has been fixed at caution and the drive rod goes to the top arm only. The lamps are the post-Grouping design with a round case manufactured by the Welch Lamp Co.
G. H. Platt/R. W. Miller Collection

Top: Ainsdale Beach station signalbox and crossing gates in January 1953. Recorded at the very end of the life of the Southport line, the painted name on the signalbox dates from the 1912 renaming! *Doug Livesey/ Author's Collection*

Left: Throstle Nest East box, an example of a large CLC signalbox constructed with standard sized panels. Photographed in April 1969, a month before closure. *S. C. Dent*

Above: The bell in the tunnel mouth at the west end of Stockport Tiviot Dale. Treadle-operated by an approaching train, it was provided to warn staff working in the vicinity. There was a similar bell at Liverpool Central. *William J. Skillern/Author's Collection*

10

Living and Working on the CLC

The range of services offered by the Cheshire Lines, coupled with its long existence, has inevitably left differing assessments of the company, from the perspective of both passengers and railwaymen. However, the overwhelming feeling from the surviving evidence is that the CLC was well liked in Cheshire and Lancashire, despite (or perhaps because of) its occasional eccentricities and foibles. It was, undoubtedly, an antiquated company by the time of nationalisation, mainly because the nature of its joint ownership militated against proper investment. Hence, although the CLC advertised itself as a modern railway, there was little to support this view outside the flagship Liverpool-Manchester expresses. For most passengers, travel on the CLC involved a trip behind a 'retired' locomotive, in outdated and dimly lit coaches, calling all too frequently at small rural stations. The experience of journeying from Manchester Central to Chester during the early years of the century was vividly captured by Eric Mason, who, although appreciative of the charming scenery around Delamere, complained that:

'The older CLC coaching stock was terrible to ride in at times; trains consisted of mixed six, eight and 12-wheeled non-corridor vehicles with very poor springing, often slack couplings with temperamental brake gear which worked in jerks. Another blight was gas lighting, poor enough when all the lamps were lit and the mantles not defective. It was very deceptive indeed; one could arrive at Central station in good time, wander along the train and select a compartment that seemed to be rather better illuminated than the others, and settle in to read the evening paper. After the train had started and covered perhaps half-a-mile, gas pressure would suddenly become reduced, sometimes to the extent of leaving only a blue glimmer, which would last until the train reached its first stop, when as if by magic the light would flare up again for the duration of the stop and then repeat the process, by almost extinguishing itself soon after restarting. No one ever seemed to explain the cause of all this... even in daylight hours reading was well nigh impossible because of the vibration; it was almost impossible to hold a book or a

Right: A New Brighton excursion train comes off the electrified MSJAR at Deansgate Junction, headed by LNER 'J39' No 2997.
G. H. Platt/
courtesy Railway Magazine

paper still enough to keep your eyes on a line of print. With the introduction of new bogie stock on the CLC after the first war, things improved considerably in general comfort, if not in speed of travel.' (*Railway World*, 1969)

Despite the improvements referred to, Mason's views were echoed in Canon Roger Lloyd's damning description of the Cheshire Lines during the interwar and postwar period:

'Few journeys are more pedestrian and have less to offer the romantic than the dozen grimy miles from Manchester Central to Hale in Cheshire. You do that pilgrimage in a peculiarly dirty and crowded Cheshire Lines train, pulled, probably, by an elderly and none too clean Great Central 4-4-0. No more depressingly workaday trains run in this country, and goodness knows there is no beauty of scenery that one should desire it.' (*The Fascination of Railways*, 1951)

Yet even Lloyd conceded that there was much of interest about this short journey and always 'some bit of railway lore to set the imagination moving', such as the lumbering limestone trains en route from Derbyshire to Northwich or the sheer volume of commuter trains rushing to and from Manchester's suburbs.

By way of contrast, passengers using the 'Punctual Route' between Liverpool and Manchester often commented on the speed and efficiency of the CLC Express, which quickly became an established favourite with commuters,

or 'contractors' as season ticket holders were known. The *Railway Magazine*, prompted no doubt by the Cheshire Lines' publicity department, suggested the alternative title of City Links City for this stretch of the CLC, and much of the Committee's publicity efforts were expended in advertising the modernity of its expresses. In a prose style so characteristic of the age, a reporter for the *Liverpool Review* summed up his journey on one such express in November 1889:

'Travelling in a luxuriant first class compartment, half buried in soft cushions, with a fine full-flavoured cigar between your teeth, and the train sailing along almost at the rate of a mile a minute, is as near an approach to a perambulating paradise as anything my mind can conceive.'

With the exception of the industrialised regions around Manchester and Liverpool, much of the CLC's network passed through lush countryside, with the Chester section particularly enjoyed for its rhododendron-lined embankments. The natural beauty of south Lancashire and Cheshire was reflected in the appearance of the Committee's wayside stations, which competed annually for the prize of best kept station and garden. For many years this title was held by Flixton and later by Barrow for Tarvin, although a study of CLC station photographs reveals the extraordinary care and attention lavished on almost every station garden by dedicated staff — a factor which surely enhanced the experience of passengers and is still remembered 60 years on by those who used the Cheshire Lines before World War 2.

While compiling this book, a number of individuals have come forward with memories of the CLC, all of them affectionate towards the company and its staff. It is easy to dismiss such reminiscences as nostalgic but that would be to ignore the very real fondness for the Cheshire Lines expressed again and again by ex-employees and passengers alike.

Mrs Betty Dutton went to school in Bowden from Hartford & Greenbank station during the 1930s and early 1940s, leaving the train at Hale. She describes Hartford & Greenbank station as:

Above: This early Edwardian view of Hale shows the magnificent, ornate canopy valances as well as the unique signalbox. In the station yard, the horse-cab carries a 'Licensed by the CLC' plate. The road surface shows one of the disadvantages of using horses as the normal motive power; at least internal combustion's pollution blows away in the wind!
E. M. Johnson Collection

Right: Knutsford station also had unusual canopies with ornate valances. It was distinguished too by the large, circular water tank on a brick tower, rather than the usual rectangular structure.
Lens of Sutton

'...so beautifully kept that it often won the best-kept station award. The staff were kindly and cheerful, taking your tickets or checking your rail contract card always with a thank you and a smile. In the waiting room was a horsehair sofa made of mahogany and a huge coal fire, where in the mornings the children finished the previous evening's homework, as they got their breath back after running so as not to miss the train. All the other stations on the line were well kept, competing with their gardens in the annual competition. Dahlias,

asters, roses, lobelia and alyssum remain in my memory and rhododendrons, laburnums and spring flowers came in their turn along the lineside.

'There were many children travelling to higher education in Hale, Altrincham, Bowden or Sale and on the return journey the girls from my school had to travel in reserved carriages at the front of the train, away from the boys who had to travel at the back of the train. The label was firmly stuck and prominently displayed on the carriage windows

and woe betide anyone who broke the segregation rules. Numerous businessmen travelled to Knutsford, Hale, Altrincham and Manchester and we children got to know their faces and mannerisms well. During the war years some of the trains from Manchester had to cease their journey to Chester at Northwich and return to Manchester, so those of us for Hartford & Greenbank would have to walk the rest of the journey home, carrying heavy school bags or a case of hard-backed text books, lacrosse sticks and tennis rackets, art portfolios and so on. Sometimes we might be fortunate enough to catch a North Western bus for part of the way. No one thought of complaining, as our minds were by then geared to the inconvenience of wartime conditions. All the nameboards were removed from the stations in case of enemy attack by parachute.'

Another reason for the fondness with which the CLC is remembered, was the part it played in conveying holidaymakers and day-trippers to their destinations. Additional to the types of excursions mentioned previously (such as the boat traffic to and from Liverpool), were the annual 'works outings' of the larger employers, which the CLC was well placed to arrange, serving as it did popular resorts such as Southport and Chester. For example, the Manchester sweet manufacturers Hall Brothers regularly organised Bank Holiday excursions with the CLC, and in August 1927 arranged for a special train hauled by no less a locomotive than *Flying Scotsman* to take its workforce from Manchester Victoria to Chester Northgate, via Stockport, Altrincham, Knutsford and Delamere. Over the years, many organisations took advantage of the service and among the CLC's varied clients were religious groups, school parties, political organisations and even a group of Winsford businessmen who, during the 1920s, booked a through train from Winsford for the annual Doncaster races.

Equally popular were the walking and cycling tours offered by the CLC in Lancashire, Cheshire, Derbyshire and North Wales, where the passenger could alight at one station and rejoin the railway at another, with road distances ranging from 5 miles to over 70, depending on the athletic abilities of the traveller. Another popular recreation was fishing, and special Anglers' Tickets were available to a wide range of destinations from all principal CLC stations. Among CLC destinations famed for fishing were Lydiate, Plumbley, Lostock Gralam and Delamere, although tickets were also issued to stations on the GNR, GCR, MR, GWR, NSR and Cambrian Railways. However, to prevent the would-be holidaymaker from taking advantage of the cheap tickets offered to anglers, a note in the 1910 *Programme of Excursion, Continental and Tourist Ticket Arrangements*, advised that such tickets would only be available on the production of 'rod and line at the time of booking [and] at the examination of Tickets and when demanded by any of the Company's servants'!

As an employer, the Committee took a paternalistic approach towards staff and sought to foster *esprit de corps* at all levels. An annual ball was held for employees at the Adelphi Hotel in Liverpool, where staff from the top level down would mingle together. Similarly, an inter-department cricket match was played at Aigburth each year, when even the lowest grade of staff would have the opportunity of bowling out the General Manager! For those of a more athletic temperament, the CLC hosted an annual 'sporting

Left: Ashley, on the Manchester-Chester line, was a nice example of a country station. It is seen in 1948, from the Chester platform, looking towards Hale. *Oliver Carter*

Right: A wonderful example of a magazine's advertising department getting it wrong. What the CLC's officers said when they saw their advert illustrated with an LNWR train can only be imagined — doubtless there were some broad grins at Euston! *Author's Collection*

THE CHESHIRE LINES PROVIDES
PUNCTUAL * SPEEDY * AND
COMFORTABLE RAIL COMMUNICATION

TO AND FROM LIVERPOOL

AND

MANCHESTER,
WARRINGTON,
CHESTER,

EXPRESS TRAINS between MANCHESTER and LIVERPOOL (Central Stations), leaving each Terminus at Half-Past every Hour from 8.30 a.m. to 9.30 p.m.

Journey in
40
Minutes.

AND

SOUTHPORT,
KNUTSFORD,
STOCKPORT.

SEASIDE EXCURSIONS AT POPULAR FARES.

THROUGH BOOKINGS TO
ISLE OF MAN, IRELAND, SCOTLAND AND NORTH WALES.

June, 1911. *For particulars apply to the Manager, Central Station, Liverpool.*

festival', inaugurated in 1882 and held alternately at grounds adjacent to the Committee's stations. According to a newspaper report of 1931, the festival was open to employees of the CLC and associated companies (ie the LMS & LNER), with prizes presented by the Manager's wife to the accompaniment of the Cheshire Lines Band.

Many of these, and other, sporting events were organised under the auspices of the Cheshire Lines Recreation and Welfare Association. In 1930 Ordinary Members (employees) and Associate Members (their families) paid a weekly subscription of 3d, which enabled them to take advantage of the sporting facilities available at the CLC's Garston Recreational Ground and also entitled them to discounted rail travel to and from the venue. To start with, as it was more convenient for many members to go direct to Liverpool and thence back to Garston on the local train, free unlimited rail travel passes were issued to members. This practice was stopped after a couple of months, killed by the number of families who took the opportunity to go shopping in Liverpool and were seen passing the ticket barriers loaded

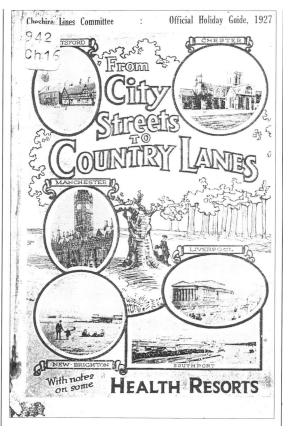

with parcels. The Association was governed by an executive committee which was part elected and part nominated by the Manager, who also acted as the Association's President. As well as sporting facilities, the Association provided evening lectures and slide shows, often presented by the Manager and covering a wide range of topics from the early history of railways through to foreign holidays. The Committee also encouraged employees to join the St John's Ambulance Association and regular classes were held at the larger stations. Once qualified, the railwayman was permitted to wear a circular nickel/enamel arm badge on his uniform, which bore the title of the company together with the cross of St John. From 1893, annual 'First Aid' displays were organised at Liverpool, with teams from all parts of the CLC competing for a silver challenge cup and a place in the national inter-railway company finals.

The staff themselves were not above having some enjoyment and small personal gain from their work on the railway. One story comes from a man who worked as a relief porter at Ashley, Hale, Baguley and Northenden and many more

stations, and it concerns Ashley station. He would always keep the coal fire burning in the waiting room so that two poachers, who regularly arrived at Ashley from Stockport on the last train on Friday, could keep warm before the first train back the next morning. In return for this kindness there was always a skinned rabbit left for him.

Mr Frank Williams, who lived for many, many years by the CLC line at Padgate station and whose father was employed by the railway as bridge painter for about 50 years, remembers an occasion when:

'Father came home with a large photograph of Furness Abbey complete with bloodstains, due to one train standing at St Michaels or possibly St James being run into the rear inside the tunnel, which caused some loss of life. The photograph was one of a series that used to adorn compartments.'

And on another occasion:

'Father and his painting gang had erected scaffolding prior to painting a bridge, when

Cheshire Lines.

☞ THE FAVOURITE ROUTE

FROM

Lancashire and Cheshire
to the North Wales Coast

IS

Via LIVERPOOL.

CHEAP EXCURSION TICKETS are issued for Half-Day, One Day, Week End, 10 or 11 Days, and for longer periods.

The Tickets are issued DAILY, Sundays included, at the undermentioned Stations.

		TO
Manchester (C.), Chorlton-c-Hardy, Urmston, Flixton, Irlam, Cadishead, Glazebrook, *Padgate, Warrington, Sankey, *Farnworth, *Hough Green, Northwich, *Knutsford, *Mobberley,	*Peel Causeway, *Altrincham, *Timperley, *Brooklands, *Sale, Stretford, *Old Trafford, *Godley, *Woodley, Stockport (Tiviot Dale), *Baguley, *West Timperley, *Southport (Lord St.) & *Birkdale.	LLANDUDNO, BANGOR, BEAUMARIS, AND MENAI BRIDGE.

*—No Bookings from these Stations on Sundays.

Popular Afternoon Trips to Llandudno

ON SATURDAYS & SUNDAYS

During the Summer Months.

For Fares, Train Service & full particulars, see Programmes issued, to be obtained Free at Cheshire Lines Stations, or from the undersigned,

Central Station, Liverpool.　　　　**DAVID MELDRUM, Manager.**

Punctual Service of Trains every 5 minutes.

Splendid View of six miles of Docks and River Frontage.

Quickest Route to all the Docks, Seaforth, Waterloo, and Great Crosby; also Prince's and Sefton Parks.

LIVERPOOL OVERHEAD ELECTRIC RAILWAY
MOVING STAIRCASE
SEAFORTH SANDS STATION

SPECIAL RATES to Large Parties of Excursionists.

RAILWAY FARES—

1st Class 3d.　2nd Class 2d.

FOR ANY DISTANCE.

3t, James Street, Liverpool.　　　S. B. COTTRELL, General Manager.

Far left: For some years the CLC's enthusiastic marketing team encouraged travel on the system with an annual *Holiday Guide. Author's Collection*

Left: Front page of the Summer 1913 timetable. Note that as a weapon in the trade war with competing companies, it was given away free; modern TOCs expect intending passengers to pay to find out when they run trains! *Author's Collection*

Above, above right & right: Another leisure promotion was the 'walking tours' tickets, which took passengers out to one station and back from another, after a scenic walk between the two.
David Bownes Collection

Below: A reminder that the railway companies had a form for almost everything. This is a voucher for re-routing a goods consignment to a station off the CLC.
Author

CHESHIRE · LINES · RAILWAY
Walking Tours
IN
CHESHIRE · LANCASHIRE · · ·
DERBYSHIRE · & · NORTH WALES

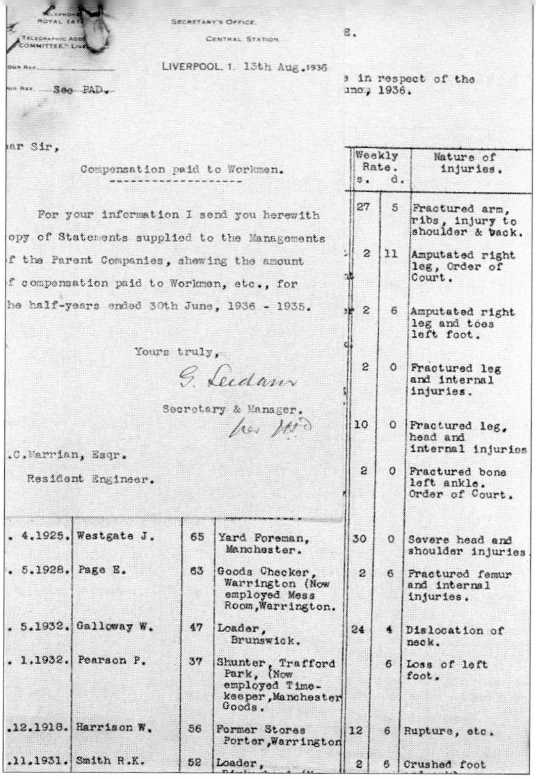

ROYAL ...
SECRETARY'S OFFICE.
CENTRAL STATION.

TELEGRAPHIC ADD...
COMMITTEE Line...

LIVERPOOL. 1. 13th Aug. 1936.

... in respect of the
... 1936.

See PAD.

... Sir,

    Compensation paid to Workmen.

For your information I send you herewith
... copy of Statements supplied to the Managements
of the Parent Companies, shewing the amount
of compensation paid to Workmen, etc., for
the half-years ended 30th June, 1936 - 1935.

Yours truly,

G. Leedam

Secretary & Manager.

.C. Marrian, Esqr.
    Resident Engineer.

Weekly Rate s.	d.	Nature of injuries.
27	5	Fractured arm, ribs, injury to shoulder & back.
2	11	Amputated right leg, Order of Court.
2	6	Amputated right leg and toes left foot.
2	0	Fractured leg and internal injuries.
10	0	Fractured leg, head and internal injuries
2	0	Fractured bone left ankle. Order of Court.

					Weekly Rate		
. 4.1925.	Westgate J.	65	Yard Foreman, Manchester.		30	0	Severe head and shoulder injuries.
. 5.1928.	Page E.	63	Goods Checker, Warrington (Now employed Mess Room, Warrington.		2	6	Fractured femur and internal injuries.
. 5.1932.	Galloway W.	47	Loader, Brunswick.		24	4	Dislocation of neck.
. 1.1932.	Pearson P.	37	Shunter, Trafford Park, (Now employed Time-keeper, Manchester Goods.			6	Loss of left foot.
.12.1918.	Harrison W.	56	Former Stores Porter, Warrington		12	6	Rupture, etc.
.11.1931.	Smith R.K.	52	Loader, ...		2	6	Crushed foot

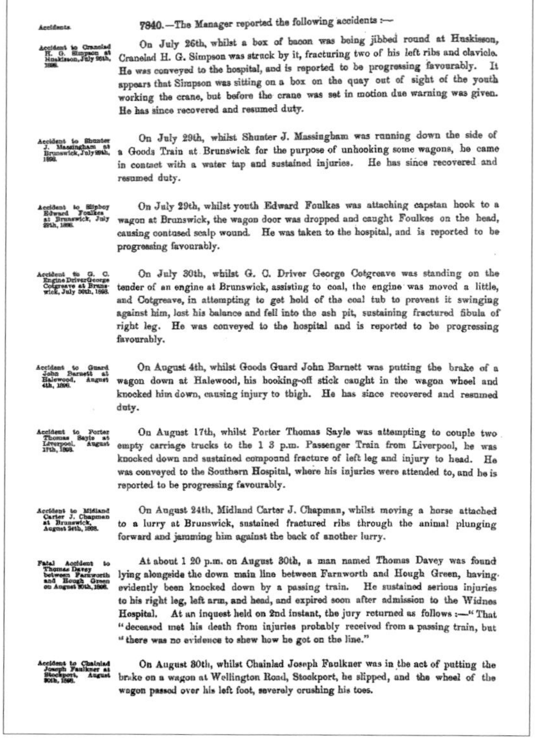

7840.—The Manager reported the following accidents :—

Accident to Craneled H. G. Simpson at Huskisson, July 26th, 1936. — On July 26th, whilst a box of bacon was being jibbed round at Huskisson, Craneled H. G. Simpson was struck by it, fracturing two of his left ribs and clavicle. He was conveyed to the hospital, and is reported to be progressing favourably. It appears that Simpson was sitting on a box on the quay out of sight of the youth working the crane, but before the crane was set in motion due warning was given. He has since recovered and resumed duty.

Accident to Shunter J. Massingham at Brunswick, July 29th, 1936. — On July 29th, whilst Shunter J. Massingham was running down the side of a Goods Train at Brunswick for the purpose of unhooking some wagons, he came in contact with a water tap and sustained injuries. He has since recovered and resumed duty.

Accident to Shipboy Edward Foulkes at Brunswick, July 29th, 1936. — On July 29th, whilst youth Edward Foulkes was attaching capstan hook to a wagon at Brunswick, the wagon door was dropped and caught Foulkes on the head, causing contused scalp wound. He was taken to the hospital, and is reported to be progressing favourably.

Accident to G. C. Engine Driver George Cotgreave at Brunswick, July 30th, 1936. — On July 30th, whilst G. C. Driver George Cotgreave was standing on the tender of an engine at Brunswick, assisting to coal, the engine was moved a little, and Cotgreave, in attempting to get hold of the coal tub to prevent it swinging against him, lost his balance and fell into the ash pit, sustaining fractured fibula of right leg. He was conveyed to the hospital and is reported to be progressing favourably.

Accident to Guard John Barnett at Halewood, August 4th, 1936. — On August 4th, whilst Goods Guard John Barnett was putting the brake of a wagon down at Halewood, his booking-off stick caught in the wagon wheel and knocked him down, causing injury to thigh. He has since recovered and resumed duty.

Accident to Porter Thomas Sayle at Liverpool, August 17th, 1936. — On August 17th, whilst Porter Thomas Sayle was attempting to couple two empty carriage trucks to the 1 3 p.m. Passenger Train from Liverpool, he was knocked down and sustained compound fracture of left leg and injury to head. He was conveyed to the Southern Hospital, where his injuries were attended to, and he is reported to be progressing favourably.

Accident to Midland Carter J. Chapman at Brunswick, August 24th, 1936. — On August 24th, Midland Carter J. Chapman, whilst moving a horse attached to a lurry at Brunswick, sustained fractured ribs through the animal plunging forward and jamming him against the back of another lurry.

Fatal Accident to Thomas Davey between Farnworth and Hough Green on August 30th, 1936. — At about 1 20 p.m. on August 30th, a man named Thomas Davey was found lying alongside the down main line between Farnworth and Hough Green, having evidently been knocked down by a passing train. He sustained serious injuries to his right leg, left arm, and head, and expired soon after admission to the Widnes Hospital. An inquest held on 2nd instant, the jury returned as follows :—" That "deceased met his death from injuries probably received from a passing train, but "there was no evidence to shew how he got on the line."

Accident to Chainlad Joseph Faulkner at Stockport, August 30th, 1936. — On August 30th, whilst Chainlad Joseph Faulkner was in the act of putting the brake on a wagon at Wellington Road, Stockport, he slipped, and the wheel of the wagon passed over his left foot, severely crushing his toes.

---

word came through that the Royal Train was due to pass underneath and instructions were given to dismantle the staging and re-erect it following the passing of the train.'

Frank Williams also recalls in an article in the now defunct magazine *Northwest Railway Enthusiast*, that on the direct line from Padgate Junction to Sankey Junction, which was used by express passenger and freight trains to avoid Warrington Central, he saw American troops, during World War 1, throwing out tins of bully beef from the carriage windows to the local residents.

As with the other large employers of the time, the influence of the CLC on the day-to-day lives of its workforce was great. Many lived in cottages built and owned by the Committee and in the early days these were nominally rent free, although the actual costs were reflected in wage levels. However, the standard of accommodation was not always what it might have been. In 1890 the stationmaster at Tiviot Dale, Mr Roberts, was given permission to live in the town at the CLC's expense, as accommodation over the station was described as 'somewhat unhealthy'. His lead was followed in 1894 by a number of stationmasters who opted to either move out of company-owned premises or pay the Committee a reasonable rent in return for better accommodation, with a suitable increase in their salaries. On average this amounted to an additional £10 per annum, although the stationmaster at Chester had £15 added to his salary, while Mr Roberts at Tiviot Dale charged the Committee £25 a year for rented accommodation in Stockport.

Mrs Moores, whose husband worked at Tiviot Dale station for 20 years as a booking clerk, remembers it as:

'A happy station with all the staff friendly and a nice refreshment room with a bar. We were married on 16 August 1926 and my husband was given two days' leave, so on the second day we went for a day trip to Southport. As we boarded the train, all the station staff stood on the platform to wish us Bon Voyage and as the train went into the tunnel several fog signals exploded.'

Mrs Moores' family was well connected with the CLC, as her husband's father was head clerk and his elder brother was in the goods section of the Stockport section of the Cheshire Lines, while his younger brother worked in head office at Manchester Central station. Mrs Moores wrote these recollections in 1996 at the age of 94, living alone as her husband had died in 1938 aged only 36 years.

In terms of pay and conditions, CLC practice was very close to the Midland, but considerably below that of the Great Central and Great Northern, both of which offered higher pay and more attractive leave entitlements to their workforces. For example, in 1898 CLC guards were not entitled to any leave with pay, whereas Great Northern guards were allowed either five or six days depending on their length of service, while the GCR offered guards four days' leave irrespective of service. Similarly, whereas shunters at the parent companies' busiest stations worked eight hour shifts, shunters on the CLC worked ten and twelve hour days. Many of these anomalies were removed following the Grouping, although pay remained low in comparison with that offered by the LMS and LNER.

Mr Ron Carey, who started as a cleaner in 1937 at Northwich Shed, became a driver in 1948 and retired in 1982. He wrote his memoirs in 1996 at the age of 76 and particularly recalled two tales of the American Army, who were stationed at Cuddington in World War 2.

'Returning from Heaton Mersey Sheds on an early morning goods train, we were stopped at Knutsford. The signalman told us that the signalman at Mobberley had seen a red glow in one of the wagons and the driver told me to go back along the train to see what it was. To my amazement I heard voices coming from the wagon, so I got up to have a look and found that there were six Americans inside smoking big cigars. Therefore the assumption had to be that the glow seen by the signalman at Knutsford had come from these cigars.'

Another episode he particularly remembers was when working a passenger train from Chester to Manchester.

'We came off the shed at Chester Northgate with an LNER tank engine that had a pull-out regulator. We backed up to the train when some American soldiers came up and exclaimed, 'Good God — a salmon tin on wheels, will it get us to Manchester?''

Mrs Doreen Jackson, the daughter of Vinson Gulliver, has several interesting stories about her father, dictated to her when he was 108 years old.

'When he started at Trafford Park Locomotive Shed, the pay for engine cleaners was 2s 6d per day for a 60-hour week. Five weeks later this was increased to 3s 0d per day and to live on this basic wage was very difficult. Able to use a pick and shovel, my father made some extra money by picking up and stacking coal, as well as working on Sundays on the coal stage on contract at 4d per ton, much of this coal being for Cunard Liners.

'At that time he regularly cleaned the locomotive *Queen Alexandra* and got such a good reputation for its cleanliness that the engine was noticed and written about. This reputation for cleaning led to him being given the nickname of Vim — 'the universal cleaner'.

Vinson Gulliver also told his daughter of 1911, a year of depression, when he was asked to help with the complete stocktaking of the CLC.

'The clerk from the ledger office was sent to find out exactly how well off the company was and in the end it was found to be in financial good order. Every nut and bolt was counted and weighed, the value was assessed everywhere. At that time the stores issuer was an old man called Austin, who claimed to have started work on the Ashton, Oldham & Guide Bridge Railway as a lad at Newton, Hyde, when that was the headquarters and the line terminated at Old Dinting. The entire number of locomotives used on the line then was 16. Vinson Gulliver's chief had an interview with him to try and establish his age and record and it was found that his story was correct and as he was willing and able to work, he was allowed to remain an employee. It was interesting to hear his stories about the railway in its infancy going back to the time when Liverpool traffic went via Timperley Junction, Lymm and Warrington Bank Quay to Garston.'

Fogs in Manchester and the surrounding areas were notorious until the advent of smokeless zones cleared them away. Again Vinson Gulliver's daughter tells the tale:

'One Christmas during World War 2 was the worst day that Father could ever remember for fog. He was on what should have been an easy diagram, relieve the 1.10pm Oldham, turn back at Trafford Park station, then take the 3.10pm to Chester and the Milk Train back. Well on this particular day it was very foggy and the train was late. Central station was in some difficulty with nothing on time. While Father was waiting at Trafford Park station, the fog came on so thick and stinking yellow that one could only just hear the engine whistle at the end of the platform. He did not know what time it was when he did his Oldham trip but when they then set off for Chester it was already late. Father and his mate knew the road very well but neither of them could see half the signal lights and so each time it was necessary to climb the posts or walk to the signalbox, whichever seemed the best, all the way to Chester. There were hardly any fog men out, as they had probably gone home being of little use. The fog men were out at Delamere all night for the first time in 20 years, although conditions were not so bad as elsewhere. They got to Chester at 12.20am and then had to get back in conditions that were no better than before. They hauled the coaches that should have left at 6.20pm for Manchester and the Milk Train as well. That meant stopping just right for the churns and the engine had to be kept really quiet so that starting could rely on the guard's whistle. So the journey went on through the night and fog, with father's mate never getting irritable but just keeping up a sober progress. The crew arrived at Old Trafford, where two truckloads were put off, at 6.30am and it was impossible to see whether one was in the tunnel or the platform as the fog was still so bad. Anyway father and his mate were near home and when he got there his face was as black as his jacket. It transpired later that his crew was one of the few to work that night.'

Let us not forget the enthusiast and those people who simply enjoyed looking at trains on the CLC. Geoffrey Collins, when a boy of 11, was so keen to watch the Cheshire Lines trains from Moss Lane Bridge by Skelton Junction signalbox, that he lingered until the Timperley police booked him for obstruction. One hopes that this was done as a joke and without any malice.

All the details of engines, buildings and line construction cannot convey the human story of working for, travelling on and spotting the CLC as eloquently as these testimonies. After all, the success of any organisation depends on its acceptance by ordinary people and a railway company, perhaps more than any other, exists to provide a service and not as an end in itself. But is must also not be forgotten that the CLC was a business and therefore had to be managed. So let us end this description of Living and Working on the CLC on a formal note.

The first meeting for the Committee of the Directors for the Cheshire Lines had taken place at Manchester London Road station on 5 November 1863 and these meetings continued at monthly intervals until the railway was nationalised at the beginning of 1948. In earlier years many of the meetings were held at King's Cross but in later years the usual venue was Marylebone. At nationalisation other railways needed a meeting for directors in 1948, to approve the final accounts for the last shareholders' meeting but the Cheshire Lines, of course, had no individual shareholders, the whole of the share capital being owned by the LMS (one third) and the LNER (two thirds). So the last CLC meeting was convened at Marylebone on Tuesday 9 December 1947, with the directors ceasing to hold office at midnight on 31 December that year.

Right: Street scene at Clubmoor on 20 August 1960, with Fairburn 2-6-4T No 42113 passing on a passenger train. *John Horne*

Below: Eastleigh-built '8F' No 48683 on a limestone train passes a foot/occupation crossing close to Cheadle. *Author*

The minutes were written up in beautiful copperplate and in all occupied 27 massive volumes. They were numbered from Number 1 in 1863 and reached Number 14,208 for the last minute of all, which read as follows:

'At this the last meeting of the Cheshire Lines Committee, the members of the Committee desire to place on record their deep appreciation of the loyal and efficient service rendered to the Committee at all times by the Secretary and Manager — Mr Gerald Leedham, his officers and staff, and to wish each and all of them success and happiness in the future. The last few years in particular have been full of difficulties and the Cheshire Lines organisation, under the inspiring leadership of Mr Leedham, has successfully surmounted each one as it arose.'

Epilogue- The CLC post - 1947

Following nationalisation of the railways with effect from 1 January 1948, since there was now no commercial logic for either Eastern or North Eastern Region involvement, it was natural for the Cheshire Lines routes to become part of the London Midland Region. Thus from 28 November 1948 the LMR assumed responsibility for the provision of motive power. As happened elsewhere on the national network, changes to regional boundaries brought an influx of locomotive types from the new regions, supplanting those of the former operating regime. Again as elsewhere, the conservative nature of CLC footplate crews did not welcome interlopers.

It is appropriate at this point to take a look at the motive power scene at this time of transition, not least because two famous locomotive types were involved. During 1947 10 of the 'D10' original 'Director' 4-4-0s moved to Brunswick and Northwich (three each) and Trafford Park, putting in appearances on the Liverpool to Manchester expresses. By October 1949 the remaining three had also migrated from Sheffield to Brunswick. No 62658 of Brunswick quickly appeared in the new BR fully lined-out livery and was something of a favourite, featuring regularly on the through Hull services. However, the class was quickly supplanted on the expresses and their final duties came on Manchester to Chester stopping trains while based at Northwich, from where eight were withdrawn.

The arrival of the 'Directors' quickly saw off the older 'D9s', of which the CLC had a total allocation of 27 in 1947. Deployment had been on all types of passenger work but their poor condition saw them struggling even on the extended schedules of the period.

Below: A Chester train runs into Manchester Central in 1964, passing under the 1930s power signalbox. 'Peak' D 149 waits with a St Pancras train on the right. *Author*

An unexpected arrival in 1949 was an ex-GER 'Claud Hamilton' 'D16/3'. Following trials, others were sent to the CLC and spent a couple of years, mainly on local trains, especially to Chester.

The year 1950 brought an influx of 'D11' 'Directors', a surprising event in view of LMR control. Heaton Mersey used its allocation to cover a turn which involved a stopping service to Liverpool and back, with a return express duty to Manchester sandwiched in between. They also took a hand on the Liverpool portion of the Marylebone to Manchester Mail, which detached at Godley. Although all 11 of the first series eventually came to the CLC, by then Stanier 'Black Fives' and Fairburn 2-6-4Ts were in charge of the principal jobs and the ex-GC type saw long periods in store, with latterly only Northwich Shed putting them to any real use. By 1958 they had all moved to Sheffield.

Although the 'J10' 0-6-0s were built as freight locomotives, post-nationalisation they were regular performers on some passenger trains over CLC metals. Notable was their use on the Wigan Extension and especially services to St Helens, on which they saw out the passenger timetable. Allocated widely across former CLC sheds, the 'J10s' were essentially the staple freight prime movers on diagrams from those depots until replaced. While never allocated to the CLC, the ex-LNER 'O4s' were a familiar sight on heavy long-distance freights. Gorton examples were frequently seen on coal traffic until it lost its last members of the class in 1962.

Turning to tank engines, the 'C13' 4-4-2Ts were very popular and coped with the Liverpool to Manchester expresses, keeping to time. Although only a few 'J39' 0-6-0Ts were actually ever on the CLC's books, by virtue of Gorton having an allocation, the type was regularly seen. As late as 1959 No 64875 worked over the CLC to Aintree Southport junction on an excursion to Southport. The 'N5s', of GCR origin, were also widely deployed across the CLC until the late 1950s. Utilisation was primarily on shunting and local goods movements but some sheds, notably Northwich, put them to use on stopping passenger turns.

After assuming control of CLC motive power, the LMR drafted in former Midland '2P' and '4P' 4-4-0s, the latter being the famous Compounds. These were heartily disliked by drivers used to ex-GCR locomotives, notably those at Trafford Park. To be fair, the new arrivals were not in the best of condition but the crews did not take to the need to learn the different driving technique that was required and they also disliked the less comfortable cab. A further problem was that the overall length of the '4Ps' exceeded the

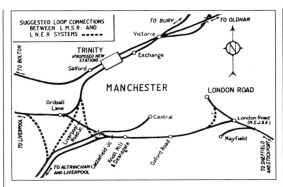

Left: About the time of nationalisation a major scheme for Manchester was drawn up, which would have seen the replacement of the four main city stations by a single new one called Trinity, with new connecting lines to link the incoming routes. Post-war economies and financial restraints killed the plan.

dimensions of Brunswick's turntable. Although both classes could be seen in use throughout the 1950s, more modern ex-LMS types soon took charge of the Liverpool to Manchester expresses; in particular, the 2-6-4Ts gradually became dominant.

Northwich received Stanier '8Fs' for the heavy chemical-related freight flows in the area. The class had a long association with the limestone workings between the Peak District and Northwich. The other ex-LMS type to be mentioned is the 2-6-2T, which replaced older machines of GCR and GNR origin. Interestingly, very few of the BR Standard engines were ever given to CLC sheds.

The transition from steam to diesel and rationalisation of routes and services, which came about largely in the 1960s, left its mark on the CLC. Allerton shed was rebuilt as a diesel and electric maintenance facility. Of the old sheds, only Northwich saw out the decade, reduced to the status of a fuelling and crew signing-on point. It became well known for a time as host to visiting steam engines running special excursions round the BR network and also played its part in the Liverpool & Manchester Railway 150th celebrations. It eventually succumbed in the mid-1980s, when changes to the traction arrangements for the ICI services meant a banking engine was no longer required from Northwich to the ICI works, and motive power was provided by Buxton instead.

On dieselisation of passenger workings the expresses were made up of two four-car sets (ie eight cars). They later became one four-car set,

then later still were reduced to only a three-car set. Suburban trains were mostly three two-car sets (ie six cars) at first but there were also some three-car sets involved to make up seven-car or five-car trains. It tends to be forgotten how long the trains were when DMUs were first enthusiastically introduced. But at a time when long through journeys across country were being axed, Liverpool lost its direct links with the East Coast.

The Beeching era had its impact on the CLC as on so many railway networks. The local passenger service, which traversed the Glazebrook to Stockport section, went on 30 November 1964. The connection from the Woodhead route at Godley to Tiviot Dale had already closed on 5 March 1962. Local services out of Manchester Central through Tiviot Dale and onwards via Romiley Junction succumbed on 2 January 1967. Some excursion traffic may well have used these

Left: Liverpool Central kept its traditional atmosphere to the very end of steam working. On 24 October 1964, in the changeover period, a two-car DMU from Gateacre is running in as sunbeams pierce the fumes above. *John Clarke*

Above right: Parts of the CLC had a long association with steam hauled specials. Here on 28 April 1979 rebuilt Bulleid Pacific No 35028 *Clan Line* brings out spectators at Altrincham as it heads a railtour between Hereford and Guide Bridge. *Tom Heavyside*

Below right: In pouring rain on 12 July 1984 Nos 20141 and 20185 pass Plumley West Signalbox with a loaded ICI hopper train. The debris on the left of the picture is the result of a serious incident some days before, when a train left the rails at this spot. *Author*

routes after the closure dates quoted, as these relate to the loss of timetable services. This also applied to the Warrington avoiding line, where services went on 3 July 1967 but the working timetables for subsequent periods showed trains still booked that way. Manchester to Chester services were diverted at Mickle Trafford from Northgate to Chester General on 6 October 1969.

Closure of Manchester Central on 4 May 1969 saw the local services to Chester and Warrington transferred to Oxford Road, while the expresses to Liverpool ran into Piccadilly. By the time of its closure on 17 April 1972, Liverpool Central retained only the Gateacre line trains, those to Warrington and Manchester having moved to Lime Street several years earlier. Passenger

facilities on the North Liverpool Extension had been progressively cut back from Southport. Timetabled services beyond Aintree ended on 7 January 1952 and these were pruned to Gateacre on 7 November 1960. Workmen's services to serve the adjacent BICC plant survived to Helsby & Alvanley until 1963.

This was truly the nadir for the CLC and from then on matters generally improved. A revamp of the Liverpool underground electric system in 1977 saw the old Central low level platforms linked to the LYR Southport electrified line, with a southern extension along the CLC surface route which reopened on 3 January 1978. Later extension of the third-rail electrification to Hunt's Cross allowed cross-platform interchange with

Above: Cressington station closed in 1972 and reopened as part of Merseyrail in 1978. Now it is faithfully restored to CLC condition. EMU No 508141 heads the 11.30 Southport to Hunt's Cross train on 3 July 1986. *Tom Heavyside*

Left: Railfreight liveried No 58042 runs round the stock of the 'Aintree Hurdler' railtour at Aintree on 27 June 1987 on what remains of the Cheshire Lines tracks. The former LYR Liverpool-Preston line is to the right. *Steve Turner*

Right: On 16 February 1996 No 56069 is about to enter British Tar Products at Cadishead to collect empty tank wagons for return to Port Clarence on Teesside in train 6E61. *Chris Dixon*

CLC line trains to Warrington and Manchester. During the 1980s the Trans-Pennine timetable via the Hope Valley was completely recast and locomotive-hauled trains using Class 31/4s provided an hourly Liverpool to Sheffield service, with most trains continuing to Hull, Cleethorpes or East Anglia. The North Trans-Pennine timetable was also altered during this period, so that services from Liverpool Lime Street to Leeds and the Northeast were rerouted over the CLC into Manchester Piccadilly instead of Victoria station. Locomotives were replaced by Class 158 Express Sprinters once these became available from 1988 onwards.

Introduction of Manchester's Metrolink tram network in 1992 involved conversion of the former MSJAR route and caused the Manchester to Chester trains to be diverted via Stockport, rejoining their old route at Deansgate Junction north of Altrincham.

As far as freight traffic was concerned, the replacement of steam saw BR Sulzer Classes 24 and 25 and English Electric Class 40 dominant, with Brush Class 47s using CLC metals most notably on coal from Yorkshire via Woodhead bound for Fiddlers Ferry power station near Warrington. Route closures to freight followed the decline in tonnage carried by the railways. Mickle Trafford to Dee Marsh was axed in 1984 but reopened for a short spell during the early 1990s until closure of Scotland's Ravenscraig steel works ended the steel flow to Shotton. A fire at Helsby West Cheshire signalbox brought a temporary

closure of the section to Mouldsworth Junction and this closure became permanent with the rerouting of the services via Chester, effective from 14 September 1991. Oil traffic on the short spur to Partington kept the route from Skelton Junction open to around 1990 but the remainder to Glazebrook East Junction had finished on 3 August 1962, due to problems with the bridge over the Manchester Ship Canal.

Hunt's Cross to Huskisson closed completely on 31 August 1976 but the other dock stations had gone by 1970. The last train to Huskisson, the daily T21 from Edge Hill, probably ran on 29 June 1975; the next day the service was cancelled. A rail strike followed immediately and National Carriers Ltd switched permanently to road haulage out of Huskisson from then on. Services over this line beyond Fazakerley South Junction to Metal Box at Aintree had ended in 1968 and the factory was then served by a connecting spur off the Bootle branch until the company ceased to use rail in the late 1980s. The threat of a tunnel collapse in Stockport severed the through route from Portwood to Cheadle Junction in May 1980. Closure of Woodhead brought the knock-on abandonment of the railway between Godley and Woodley in 1981.

Following privatisation, freight activity is currently going through a dynamic phase, with the gradual increase in movements being seen nationwide also reflected on the old CLC. Arrival of the new General Motors Class 66 diesels is likely to have a significant impact on the motive

Left: 5D37 — the Saturdays Only 08.35 Chester to Stockport ECS, where it becomes 1D37, the SO 10.37 Stockport to Holyhead service, is headed by No 37142 in Dutch livery as it passes Northwich on 20 July 1996. *John P. Robinson*

Centre left: Extensive repairs have been necessary to Bridge 194 at Irlam. The first of the two approach spans was removed over the weekend of 26/27 April 1998. This photograph, taken with full permission and under escort, shows a Central Train — Class 158 Unit No 158780 — on a Liverpool Lime Street service on 28 April 1998. *Chris Dixon*

Below left: The 13.55 First North Western Trains service from Liverpool Lime Street to Warrington Central passes Allerton Junction on 10 March 1999, formed of Pacer No 142023. *Brian Morrison*

Right: Manchester Central's train shed has survived, transformed into the GMex exhibition centre, and rail transport of a different kind now runs just outside. Almost on the alignment of the old tram route, Metrolink tram No 1008 heads for Piccadilly on 9 June 1998. *Ken Kay*

power found in the area. The core traffic continues to be the two daily stone trains from the ICI quarry at Tunstead to either Lostock Works or Oakleigh sidings (for Wallerscote and Winnington Works). For many years these have been the only services to run on 26 December. Oakleigh sidings continue to receive coal deliveries but the service has varied over the years and at the time of writing is from the Ayrshire Coalfield. While the stone terminal at Portwood has closed, the one at Bredbury receives deliveries from Tunstead. Also at Bredbury, the refuse terminal despatches containers to Roxby near Scunthorpe.

A Hull (Saltend) to Mostyn (Deeside) chemical train joins the CLC at Northenden Junction and traverses the full length of the surviving system to Mickle Trafford. Stone from Penmaenmawr is routed to the Civil Engineer's depot at Guide Bridge this way, as are the Penyfford to Healey Mills coal empties. Other flows which use the CLC for part of their journey are the former Enterprise service from Warrington Arpley to Middlewich and the DRS-operated Sellafield to Sandbach.

On the Liverpool to Manchester route, rail activity associated with Trafford Park has seen an increase, notably following the opening of the Channel Tunnel. The route was electrified out of Manchester to avoid the need for a traction change, and carries freightliner and wagon load movements in addition to the Tunnel activity. Glazebrook continues to receive oil from Port Clarence or Lindsey refineries.

Looking to the future, it may well be that the Channel Tunnel will play an even more important part in traffic flows from the old CLC. There is serious discussion of a new line linking Liverpool with the Tunnel. It would be built to the Continental loading gauge (Berne Gauge) as was the GCR extension, part of the Watkin master plan. Promoted by Central Railways, it could follow the ex-CLC route to Manchester, then join the former GCR Woodhead line over the Pennines to Penistone. From there it would follow the Midland main line from Sheffield through to London and from there via Croydon and Ashford to reach the Channel Tunnel and Northern France. If this comes to pass then at last, many years later, Sir Edward Watkin's dream would be fulfilled, with Manchester, Liverpool and the catchment area of the CLC linked to Europe by rail.

Bibliography

Source Material
Public Record Office
Cheshire Record Office
Manchester Central Reference Library
Greater Manchester Record Office
National Railway Museum Reading Room
Private Collections

Books Used and Recommended for Further Reading

A Regional History of the Railways in Great Britain, Vol. 10, G. O. Holt, David and Charles (1978)

An Illustrated History of The Cheshires Lines Committee, Paul Bolger, Heyday Publishing Co (1984)

British Railway History, Hamilton Ellis, George Allen and Unwin (1954/59), Vol 1 1830-1876, Vol 2 1877-1947

British Railcars 1900 to 1950, D. Jenkinson & B. C. Lane, Atlantic (1996)

British Main Line Services in the Age of Steam, 1900-1968, M. Harris, Oxford Publishing Company (1996)

Cheshire Lines Committee Signal Box Register, M. J. Addison & J. G. Dixon, Privately printed (1996)

Express Trains, English and Foreign, E. Foxwell and T. C. Farrer, London (1899)

Great Central, 3 Vols, G. Dow, Locomotive publishing Co (1959 onwards)

Great Railway Stations of Britain, G. Biddle, David & Charles (1986)

J. G. Robinson — A Lifetime's Work, David Jackson, Oakwood Press (1996)

Locomotives of the Great Central Railway, E.M.Johnson, Irwell Press (1989/92) Vol 1 1897-1914 and Vol 2 1912 to British Railways

Locomotives of the LNER, The Railway Correspondence & Travel Society in 19 parts from 1973 to 1994

Man of the Rail, A. J. Pearson, George Allen & Unwin, (1967)

Manchester, Alan Kidd, Keele University Press (second edition 1996)

Passengers No More, Gerald Daniels & L. A. Dench, Ian Allan Ltd., (second edition 1973)

Plumley Station, D. M. Bownes, Privately printed (1998)

Points and Signals — A Railway Historian at Work, Michael Robbins, George Allen & Unwin (1967)

Rail Centres: Manchester, S. Hall, Ian Allan Publishing (1995)

Railway Men, Politics and Money — The Great Age of Railways in Britain, Adrian Vaughan, John Murray (1997)

Railway Scrap Book, E. W. P. Veale, Railway Publications Ltd (1962)

Railways and Waterways in Warrington, A. Norton, Cheshire Libraries & Museums (second edition 1984)

Railways of the Macclesfield District, B. Jeuda (1984)

Railwayman's Gallery, R. Lloyd, George Allen & Unwin (1953)

Railways of Marple and District from 1794, W. R. Burton, M. T. & W. R. Burton Marple (1980)

Roads and Rails of Manchester, J. Joyce, Ian Allan Ltd (1982)

Stockport Tiviot Dale — A Cheshire Line Remembered, G. K. Fox, Foxline Publishing (1991)

The Cheshire Lines Committee, Then and Now, N. F. W. Dyckhoff, Ian Allan (1984)

The Cheshire Lines Railway, R. Prys Griffiths, Oakwood Press (1947, reprinted 1958 & 1978)

The Diaries of Absalom Watkin, A Manchester Man 1787-1861, Ed Magdalen Goffin, Alan Sutton Publishing(1993)

The First Fifty Years of Brunner Mond & Co, Anon (1923)

The Great Northern Railway, 3 Vols, J. Wrottesley, B. T. Batsford (1979 & 1981)

The Harmonious Blacksmith: Robinson, Vol I The Charles Reddy Drawings, The Stephenson Locomotive Society (1995)

The LMS & LNER in Manchester, R. E. Rose, Ian Allan Ltd (1987)

The London & North Western Railway, A History, M. C. Reed, Atlantic Transport Publishers (1996)

The Midland Railway; Its Rise and Progress, Frederick S. Williams, Stranhan & Co, (second edition 1876)

The Railways of England, W. M. Ackworth, John Murray (1889)

The Railways of the Manchester Ship Canal, D. Thorpe, Oxford Publishing Company, (1984)

In addition articles were consulted in the following magazines:
Railway Magazine
Railway & Travel Monthly
The Journal of the Railway & Canal Historical Society
The Mancunian, (the journal of the Manchester Locomotive Society)
The Liverpool Review
Railway World
Backtrack
LMS Magazine
LNER Magazine
Steam Days
The Model Engineer